D0402158

Three Faces of Jesus

How Jews, Christians, and
Muslims See Him

Josef Imbach

translated from the German by
Jane Wilde

Templegate Publishers

ISBN 0-87243-194-0

Templegate Publishers
302 East Adams Street
P. O. Box 5152
Springfield, Illinois 62705

Table of Contents

Introduction

Before the orthodox Jew begins his morning prayers, he puts on his phylactery. This has small capsules attached to it which contain four texts from the bible written on parchment strips (Ex 13. 2-10; 11-16; Deut 6. 4-9; 11. 13-21). These capsules are fastened to the forehead and left arm, on the side of the heart, by the phylactery straps. Before a Muslim says his obligatory prayers five times a day, he spreads a carpet or a piece of clothing or something similar on the floor and kneels down on it.

A Christian might well shake his head at this behavior as strange to him. He is often not aware that in Judaism these texts from the Bible are to be taken literally, the point being that God's great actions to his people are written in their hearts and on their foreheads and bound to their wrists (Ex 13. 9, 16: Deut 6. 8; 11. 18). It is also likely that a Christian is just as unfamiliar with Islamic prayer rules, according to which a place of worship must be prepared by laying a carpet on the floor when it is not possible to go to the mosque. How many Christians have ever given a thought to the idea that perhaps their religious beliefs and practices of worship are also incomprehensible to members of another faith? For example how do Jews and Muslims react at the sight of a Catholic who goes into church on a Saturday afternoon, dips his hand into a basin of water, touches his forehead, chest (or belly), and shoulders with his wet fingers, bends one knee quickly to the ground, and then makes his way into a dark box to pay a short visit to a man shut up in it?

The more one unquestionably affirms one's own beliefs the more foreign one is likely to find both the religious practices and the religious convictions of others. But is there actually such a thing as a faith which will not permit questioning? Does a Christian really take it as self-evident that the salvation of the whole of mankind at any given time should be linked, of all people, to the carpenter's son from Nazareth, the back of beyond, who managed to win over a couple of Galilean fishermen who then took to their heels after his deplorable failure and fled? Certainly one can and should ask how this particular bungler could have been proclaimed the Messiah and Redeemer of all mankind

5

so soon after his shameful death on the cross. Or can it be that it is precisely in this way that the truth of Christianity is demonstrated? The followers of Judaism continue to wait for the Messiah with undiminished hope, and Muhammad founded a new religion almost six hundred years after Christ's death, which at times spread just as rapidly as Christianity, and whose truth for the Muslims is unquestionable.

Each of the three great monotheistic religions has crucial grounds for justification which—at least from the point of view of their adherents—cannot really be refuted. Gotthold Ephraim Lessing (1729-1781) alludes to this in his famous parable of the rings in "Nathan the Wise" (Act 111. sc.7.); in the end, these three religions are only different historical concrete forms of human piety. He compares belief in God to a ring which is passed from father to son through the generations.

> Then came this ring, from son to son
> At last to father of three sons,
> All three obeyed him equally,
> All three it follows he loved equally
> And could not loose himself from them.
> From time to time, he often found
> Each child alone with him,
> And then, his generous heart
> Not 'twixt the other two divided,
> It seemed first one
> And then the other, then the third
> Worthier the ring: which
> He, in pious weakness had to each
> Son promised. This state went on
> As long as it could go. But then
> His hour came round, and he was in
> Perplexity. It pained him so
> To grieve two of the three—
> All trusted in his word.
> What could he do?
> In secret sent he for a jeweller;
> Two other rings he ordered
> In shape and pattern as his own,
> No cost or effort to be spared

6

To make the copies congruent.
Success attended on the jeweller.
And when he gave the father back
His own true ring, he could himself
Not tell it from the other two.
Joyfully he called in turn
His sons, gave each in turn
His blessing and his ring;
And then he died.

What follows now was bound to come.
Scarce was the father dead, and each
Son with his ring will each be ruler
Of the house. In vain all quarrels
Questioning and blame — the father's
Ring could not be proved. Almost
As hard it is for us to prove
The one true faith.

In the end, can we come to terms with this question of belief? Can the whole of human life be based upon a "perhaps," which, if one thinks ahead consequentially, affects not only the truth of one's own religion, but of every religion ("None of your three rings is genuine") and furthermore, affects even their foundation — the very existence of God? Do we not rather seek certainties worth living — and dying for?

These questions and their respective problems will be examined in detail in this book. The reader cannot fail to notice that the author argues the phenomenon of religion and concrete religious manifestations from a Christian point of view, but in a very factual manner. Objectivity is achieved not simply by eliminating one's own assumptions of thought and personal convictions (which is not possible), but by remaining conscious of them.

This book is mainly concerned with the status of Jesus in the three great monotheistic religions. The fact that Jesus from the Christian viewpoint represents the fullness of God's revelation gives rise to a vast number of questions which are dealt with, at least in passing, in the first and the last two chapters: what is the connection between the claim to absolutism of Christianity as "the one true religion" and the absolutist ways and methods by which it constantly seeks to impose this claim

7

(thus betraying the intentions of its founder)? Does the divine image of Jesus really differ so radically from his image in Judaism and in Islam? Is Jesus in fact the "one mediator between God and men" (1 Tim 2.5), when there is also genuine — and that implies divine — revelation in other religions?

This book has had to confine itself only to what is essential, because there is no one Judaism, no one Christianity and no one Islam. To some degree extremely varied directions and movements exist within these religions themselves, which a summarizing, comparative overview cannot possibly take into account. And it is with just such an overview, which does not pursue apologetics or polemics but seeks to offer information and orientation, that we are here concerned. Both *the differences in teaching* and, within the realms of the possible, developments *within the teachings* will be incorporated.

Only a closer acquaintance with other religions makes it possible for us to revise our judgement and correct misunderstandings. Apart from this, a confrontation with other points of view enables us to contribute a great deal towards a better understanding of our own position. Naturally dialogue between the religions can only exist in an atmosphere of tolerance, in which it is assumed that one will go out to meet unfamiliar convictions with that same open-mindedness towards others that one expects for oneself, and that one will also respect the convictions of those who think differently, even when one cannot share them.

1 From Polemic to Dialogue

The ecumenical decree "Unitatis redintegratio" (issued on November 21, 1964), the declaration of the relationship of the Church to non-christian religions "Nostra aetate" (October 28, 1965) and the declaration of religious freedom "Dignitatis humanae" (December 7, 1965) are among the most remarkable documents of the Second Vatican Council.

What could be termed a prelude to these documents, the founding of the Secretariat of Unity (Segretario per l'unità dei cristiani) by Pope John XXIII on June 5, 1960 aimed to nurture and deepen the relationship between the Catholic Church and the other Christian confessions. The founding of two further secretariats by Pope Paul VI on January 6, 1966 served to corroborate and deepen the Council's resolutions. One of the secretariats aimed to provide an institutional basis for dialogue with non-Christians, the other for discussions with non-believers.

The historical importance of these theoretical announcements and their practical provisions only become really clear when one makes a comparison with the past. Pope Pius XI, in his encyclical of 1928 "Mortalium animos" described with little respect those who were interested in ecumenicism as "panchristiani," which can most accurately be translated as "commonplace Christians." The Church law first proclaimed in 1917 and valid until the appearance of the new codex in 1983, forbade Catholics to take part in religious discussions with non-Catholics without permission from the pope or the appropriate bishops (can. 1325 par. 3).

The "Syllabus" published by Pius IX in 1864 (a kind of list of "modernist errors") proclaimed that the opinion that men are at liberty to profess any religion if they are convinced of its truth, is heretical (DS 2915).[1] In his pastoral letter "Quanta cura" the same Pope announced in the same year that the call for freedom of conscience and religious worship was incompatible with church teaching (D 1690). He was referring expressly to the 1832 encyclical "Mirari vos arbitramur" of Pope Gregory XVI, in which the latter had denounced the right to freedom of conscience as "an absurd point of view, or even insane" (absurda ac erronea sententia seu potius delireamentum; DS 2730) and as "an extremely pernicious error" (pestilentissimus error; DS 2731). Certainly

9

these statements resulted from the demand for an extreme ethical autonomy of human reason and referred to modern indifference. But this does not excuse the unconcerned attitude of church teaching and its blindness towards the dignity of the human conscience.

The line from Gregory XVI can be traced straight back to Leo X, who in his papal bull "Exurge Domine" of 1520 qualified a group of Martin Luther's sentences as incompatible with Catholic belief — amongst others (and here the reader is not the victim of an optical illusion) the reformer's statement that it was against the will of God to burn heretics (DS 1483).

From today's point of view it is understandable that people were reluctant to place their church at the disposal of dissenters for the spread of their own teachings, just as Luther at one time would never have dreamt of allowing Catholic priests to preach before a Protestant congregation in compliance with an "exchange of pulpit." The fact that the faithful were warned against contact with "false teachers" is also understandable, indeed comprehensible today. But the decision of the Third Lateran Council of 1179, which forbade the faithful on pain of interdict (sub anathemate prohibemus) to grant these false teachers lodgings in their houses, to linger on their property or even to do business with them seems — to put it mildly — somewhat strange (D 401). In contrast to a broadly accepted view, the embargo was not Napoleon's invention.

If, however, we go back a little further into history, we cannot simply leave it at the fact that those among the faithful who did not unreservedly accept the official teaching were banned from the church community. We should not underestimate the power that binding and loosing had over the masses (Mt 18.18). The curse attached to excommunication was as awe-inspiring as it was terrible. The formulae used for it stem largely from the church criminal laws of the Middle Ages. The following example illustrates what the term "Anathema sit" (he is anathema; he is banned from the church) originally meant, or at least implied:

> "In the authority of Almighty God, the Father, the Son and the Holy Spirit, as in the holy canon, the holy and undefiled Virgin and Mother of God, all the heavenly hosts, the angels, archangels, thrones, dominions, powers, cherubim and seraphim, the holy patriarchs, prophets, all

10

the apostles and evangelists, the holy innocents, who alone were found worthy to sing the new song before the Lamb, the holy martyrs, the holy confessors, and the holy virgins and all the saints and the chosen of God together excommunicate and curse this thief or evildoer, and we banish him from the threshold of God's holy Church, so that for his torment he shall be seized by everlasting punishment with Dathan and Abiron and those who here said to our Lord and God: Retreat from us, for we do not wish the knowledge of thy ways. As fire is quenched by water, so shall his light be quenched for ever, unless he reflects and does satisfaction. Amen. May God curse him, the Father who created men; may the Son of God curse him, he who suffered for men; may the Holy Spirit curse him, who is poured out in baptism. May the Holy Cross curse him, which Christ, in his triumph over his enemies ascended for our salvation. May the holy Mother of God and the perpetual Virgin Mary curse him, may the holy Michael who is the escort of the holy souls curse him; may all the angels and archangels curse him, the dominions and powers and the whole militia of the heavenly army. May the holy John, the forerunner and great baptizer of Christ curse him. May the holy Peter, the holy Paul, the holy Andrew, all Christ's apostles curse him, also the other disciples, also the four evangelists who converted the whole world through their preaching. May the magnificent host of martyrs and confessors, who were found well-pleasing (to God) for their good works curse him. May the choirs of holy virgins curse him, who for the sake of Christ's honor abhorred the vanities of this world. May all the saints curse him, who from the beginning of the world through all eternity have appeared beloved of God. May heaven and earth and all that is holy within them curse him. May he be cursed wherever he finds himself, at home, in the field, on the road, on the field path, in the forest, in water, in the church. May he be cursed when he dies, when he eats, when he drinks, when he hungers or thirsts, when he fasts, when he falls asleep, when he slumbers, when he is awake, when he goes, when he stands, when he sits, when he lies, when

11

he works, when he rests, when he urinates, when he defecates, when his blood is let. May he be cursed in all the members of his body. May he be cursed inside and outside, in his hair cursed, in his brain cursed, in his hair part cursed, in his temples cursed; in his forehead, in his ears, in his eyebrows, in his eyes, in his cheeks, in his chin, in his nostrils, in his incisors, in his molars, in his lips, in his gullet, in his wrists, in his arms, in his hands, in his fingers, in his breast, in his heart, in all his entrails down to his stomach, in his kidneys, in his flanks, in his thighs, in his genitals, in his hips, in his knees, in his legs, in his feet, in his ankles, in his toenails. May he be cursed in all the ligaments of his limbs, from the crown of his head to the soles of his feet may there be no health in him. May Christ, the Son of the living God, with the whole power of his majesty curse him; may heaven rise up against him with all the might which it moves in order to damn him, if he does not do penance and give satisfaction. Amen, so may it be, so may it be. Amen."[2]

Doubtless the church teaching body had not only the right but also the duty to keep watch over the teaching of the faith. Of necessity it follows that this teaching body would dispute someone being a member of the communion of the faithful who had deviated from the basic issues of this teaching. To be more exact: the teaching body laid down that anyone who *obstinately*[3] supported serious falsehoods, put himself outside the bounds of the church.

In our way of looking at the problem of religious freedom and freedom of conscience we must be aware that the further we go back into history, the more united is the power of the church, and the more intolerant her attitude becomes towards dissenters. This intolerance, to whose theological roots we will return, was first effective at the level of church teaching, which then formed the theoretical basis for the attempt at a practical enforcement of the claim for undivided allegiance.

Some historical examples enable us to illustrate this: the persecution of the Jews, the war against the Muslims and the ruthless elimination of dissenters.

It is widely held that the antagonistic attitude of the Church towards the Jews can be traced back to the New Testament. Paul is predominantly referred to[4] because he has often been accused of creating the theological basis of the Church's anti-Jewishness through his rejection of the (Jewish) "Laws" in favor of those of "Christ" (Gal 2.21) or, on another level, through the teaching of justification, not from the "Works" prescribed by the Law, but solely through "Faith" (Rom 3.27ff). But such accusations are devoid of any basis. They overlook the fact that Paul, although he repeatedly speaks of the "hardening" of Israel (compare amongst others Rom 10.2 ff; 18 ff), never excludes his people from messianic salvation — on the contrary, he is convinced that "all Israel will be saved" (Rom 11.26), and that the "hardening" of a *part* of Israel will only last "until the full number of the Gentiles come in and so all Israel will be saved" (Rom 11.25). Paul also develops the basic theories of his laws and teachings of justification (Gal 2.11-21) *not against the Jews* but against those fellow-Christians who hold the view that baptized gentiles should be circumcised and must live according to Jewish rule of law. It is a fact that Paul never uses the term "Jew" in an anti-Jewish sense.

This is less clear in St John's gospel, where the Jews are frequently referred to in a negative way. But only single representatives of the Jewish people are implied; the pharisees and high priests (compare Jn 7.13 with 7.32); the pharisees and teachers of the law (compare 9.18 with 9.13, 15, 16); the members of the Jewish central authorities (10. 31, 39); (these references only make sense when those who are here called "Jews" hold police authority); the opponents from the leading classes (19.15,38. 20.19); the holders of power who wanted to eliminate Jesus and for *this reason* are described as "the devil's sons" (compare 8.44 with 8.37, 40); the members of the Sanhedrin (that is, of the high council; 18.35). And finally, Jesus's sermon on "the bread from heaven" (6.22-59) does not deal with a repetition of an historical event, but reflects the inner religious situation at the time of the writing of the gospel. "The Jews" here do not represent the Jewish people but the op-posing party, against whose too intellectualized interpretation the author had to defend the "real presence" (as we would say today) of Christ in the eucharistic bread. A thorough analysis of the concept "Jews" in the fourth gospel reveals that here the Jews are equated with the ruling classes, and particularly with the members of the temple aristocracy. The Church has subsequently overlooked these facts and applied terms such as (God's) murderers (8.40) and "devil's sons" (8.44) to all Jews.

It was believed that the foundation and justification for this attitude could be traced back to another source, the so-called curse of the Jews upon themselves, which is only found in Matthew: "So when Pilate saw that he was gaining nothing, but rather that a riot was beginning, he took water and washed his hands before the crowd, saying 'I am innocent of this man's blood; see to it yourselves.' Then all the people answered, 'His blood be on us and on our children' " (Mt 27.24 ff). It is this statement that has made it possible for Christians over centuries to persecute the whole Jewish people as "God's murderers," and to qualify the injustice inflicted upon them as the punishment of God. Historically seen however, it is highly unlikely that Pilate, as the representative of the Roman state control, would present his judgement as judicial murder to a subject people. It is also unthinkable that all the Jews present in Jerusalem on the occasion of the Paschal feast, let alone "all the people" were gathered before Pilate. And how should this statement be understood, if not as an historical account?

Matthew's gospel was written after the Romans, in 70 AD, had caused a fearful blood bath in Palestine and destroyed Jerusalem. It is more than probable that the evangelist connects this national catastrophe with the rejection of Christ by the Jewish people. Accordingly, cursing themselves would not have been an historical event, but a theological interpretation of the destruction. In this connection Franz Mußner has observed: "No Christian can, with a clear conscience, call upon Mt 27.25 to justify his anti-Jewishness. If Jesus' blood is upon the children of Israel, it is upon them as the blood of the Redeemer."[5]

It is precisely this fact that Christianity has either not recognized at all or frequently overlooked — with the result that the Church has been an accomplice during the many centuries of the Jewish people's suffering. *An accomplice;* for it is known that there was a pre-Christian anti-Jewishness linked to the religious non-conformism of the Jews, which, of necessity, also made a political impact in, for example, the rejection of the cult of the gods and emperors. Incidentally, on this point the Christians of the first three hundred years do not differ from the Jews — that is why they were described as *átheoi* — godless. But Christianity had scarcely been declared the state religion of the Roman Em-

14

pire when those who had previously been persecuted themselves became persecutors. Through state and church laws (or, in view of the nascent alliance of the time between the throne and the altar, better expressed as state-ecclesiastical laws), the Jews became, in the course of time, practically without rights. On the one hand there were popes like Gregory I (the Great, 540-604 AD) who practised a moderate policy towards the Jews, but on the other hand, it is thought-provoking that the Arab conquest of Spain in 711 AD was looked upon by the Jews there as a liberation.

The first Christian emperors after Constantine had already subjected the Jews to legal restrictions. They were forbidden to keep Christian slaves or to enter into marriage with a Christian (Constantius, 339). In 404 AD Honorius excluded them from military service and Theodosius II from any kind of official position. Later they had to wear special dress. From the 11th century on they were forced into ghettos, a measure which the Third Lateran Council attempted to enforce permanently in 1179. The term ghetto, however, was first used in 1516, when the Jews of Venice—in that part of the city in which the new foundry, the ghetto nuovo, was located—were resettled. In 1248-50 when the bubonic plague was raging across wide areas of Europe, the Jews were accused of poisoning the wells. Added to this there were many rumors and calumnies, as groundless as they were persistent, which lasted for centuries: the Jews would violate crucifixes, desecrate hosts, slaughter Christian children for ritualistic purposes...

Such slanders cost countless Jews their lives. In passing it should be mentioned that even the Reformation did nothing to ameliorate the situation. Even if during his early years Luther disapproved of the previous treatment of the Jews ("that Christ was a Jew by birth"; 1523), twenty years later ("Of the Jews and their lies"; 1543), disappointed that the Jews refused to convert to Christianity, he demanded the destruction of their houses, the burning of synagogues, the confiscation of their sacred texts, and the forbidding of services under pain of death.

Although Humanism, the Enlightenment and the French Revolution introduced civil equality for the Jews, they were unable to overcome those anti-Jewish feelings which assumed such demonic proportions in the Holocaust of our century.

How was all this possible? This question does not interest us here from the historical, psychological, or sociological aspects—although these are also of importance in our attitude towards the problem. How was all this possible in a society which had grown from the soil of Christianity? Hans Küng observes:

> "We ask simply as Christians, as members of a community which — unlike God's people of old — calls itself God's new people. We cannot ask this question without being struck dumb with shame and guilt. Can we indeed still want to speak, when millions have been silenced? We attempted to argue *morally* in order to justify ourselves in shameful or shameless apologetic — ("the Jews have also made mistakes" — Certainly!) or *historically* ("one must understand everything in relation to the times" — Everything?) or *theologically* ("that was not really the True Church" — Who and where is this True Church?), or *politically* ("one has to weigh it up, it was more opportune to do nothing about it" — Was it also Christian, evangelical?). How far can such self-justification go, with such an immeasurable leaden weight of guilt? The Church preached love and sowed murderous hate, she heralded life and spread the bloodiest death. And this upon the very brothers of him from whom she had heard: "Truly, I say to you, as you did it to one of the least of these my brethren, you did it to me" (Mt 25.40). The Church stood between Israel and Jesus and hindered Israel from recognizing him as its Messiah."[6]

Of course this does not imply that the entire history of the sufferings of the Jewish people under the Nazis can be blamed on the Church. But this history of suffering is unthinkable without the prehistory of anti-Jewishness, which was not only tolerated, but also practised by the Church over the centuries.

In view of this fact, the Church has emphatically admitted her guilt in the Council's declaration on her relationship to non-Christian religions: "Conscious of the heritage which she has in common with the Jews, the Church, which condemns all persecutions against any people, laments, not for political reasons but from the impetus of the religious love of the gospels, all outbreaks of hatred, persecutions and manifestations of anti-Semitism, which have been directed at any time and by any one against the Jews." (No. 4)

The same statement also emphatically retracts the assertion which was widely used in sermons and catechesis over the centuries, that the

Jews are God's murderers and as such are cursed by him. "Although the Jewish authorities with their followers urged the death of Christ (Jn 19.6), one can neither lay the blame for the fact that he suffered upon all Jews alive at the time, nor indiscriminately upon Jews today. Certainly the Church is God's new people, but even so, the Jews may not be represented as being rejected or cursed by God as if this were according to the scriptures. Everybody should be responsible for seeing that no one in catechesis or in preaching the word of God should teach anything that is not in accordance with the truth of the evangelists and the spirit of Christ" (No. 4). It should also be remembered that as early as 1959 John XXIII had struck the intercession for "the perfidious Jews" *(pro perfidis Iudaeis)* out of the Good Friday liturgy because of its insulting nature.

Simultaneously the Council has taken thought of "the shared spiritual inheritance of both Jews and Christians" and means to "promote mutual knowledge and respect, which above all will be the fruit of biblical and theological studies as well as of brotherly discussion" (No. 4). Dialogue instead of polemic, rapprochement instead of ostracism, understanding instead of rejection — if this program is really followed through, then a new age of co-existence between Jews and Christians will have truly begun.[7]

Wars Against Those of Other Faiths

The countless persecutions of those of other faiths and the numerous wars waged against the "Unbelievers" — as the Muslims were termed from the Middle Ages to the age of Humanism — belong to the darkest chapters of church history. Generally the religious wars or wars of faith are known as crusades. But in the end this term implies nothing other than the spread of the faith by the sword. Originally the desire for conquest of the occidental states in the Orient played no significant role. What was decisive was the ideal of piety held by the orders of knights from the 10th to the 13th centuries. The old Germanic conception of fealty towards the sovereign ruler was applied to the "liege lord" Christ. It was necessary to defend his affairs and to assure them of victory. The contemporary poems of chivalry express this most clearly. Remember "Chanson de Roland," "Heliand" and Wolfram von Eschenbach's

"Parzival." The powerful attraction of this ideal of piety was even a surprise to Pope Urban II. When the Byzantine Emperor asked the former for help, and when in November 1095 at the Synod at Clermont in the Auvergne the Pope called upon the Christian world to free the Holy Sepulchre, the cry "Deus vult" (God wills it) rang out on every side. Within a year an army of about 30,000 strong was ready, and it advanced on Jerusalem by way of Constantinople, Asia Minor and Syria. In 1099 the city was taken—and a terrible bloodbath was ordered.

This event was typical of the entire movement of the crusades, which lasted until the end of the 13th century. The religious motives retreated gradually into the background; it became harder to see the spreading of the faith as the original motive. Flagrant material interests and political considerations determined these crusades perhaps not exclusively, but to a very large extent.

The writing of church history, prudently glossing over and harmonizing, has often tried to "explain away" the cruelties and atrocities practised by Christians as deriving from the Zeitgeist of the time, and thus to excuse them. This is not really possible because at least during phases which were progressive, the conviction was broadly held that one should not, at any price, spread faith in Christ by force. An example of this is Francis of Assisi, who in 1219, during the fifth crusade, forced his way unarmed into the middle of the Sultan's camp in Damietta, Upper Egypt, in order to preach the faith to him and to negotiate for peace. Naturally the Papal Delegate, Cardinal Pelagius Galvan, reacted most disapprovingly to this plan. For him the crusade was the carrying out of the divine will—he could appeal to the Fourth Lateran Council (1215) for confirmation of this. Francis however persisted in his plan, so that the Cardinal finally allowed him to seek out the Sultan in his army's camp. Although he was not converted the Sultan became his firm friend. The discrepancy between the action of the little son of an Assisi merchant and the pretensions of the Church could not have been greater: while the crusaders wanted to conquer a country, Francis tried to convert a people.

The concept of non-violent spread of the faith also came to fruition, even if in a totally misdirected way, in the Children's Crusade of 1212 when thousands of children from Germany and France set off, only to be sold finally into slavery or into brothels, if indeed they had not already succumbed to the exertions of the journey.

During the crusades it was not only the Muslims who were fought, but also heretical movements within the Church—that of the Albigensians for example. According to their teaching, the world was the work of evil. Only complete abstinence from worldly concerns could lead to salvation. This movement spread widely from the town of Albi (hence the name Albigensian) and was particularly strong in Southern France in the middle of the 12th century. Neither St Dominic nor the legates sent by Innocent III from 1198 on were able to achieve much. When one of these, Peter of Castelnau, was murdered in 1208, Innocent called for a crusade against the Albigensians. This war (1209-29) had devastating effects. The Albigensians were ruthlessly exterminated and the whole of Southern France was laid waste. Even with all justifiable criticism of the means used (would Jesus have used force against one of his followers, would he have actually murdered an opponent?) one must assume that the Pope meant only to guard the Church against false teaching.

During the Turkish Wars of the 15th century, however, although there was a religious motivation (as Pius II indicated in a public speech in 1452) there was as well a strong political interest at work. Its aim was to put a brake on the Ottomans' attempts at expansion. And since the Reformation, "religious wars" have hardly ever been determined by religious motives but by political ones (the Huguenot Wars, 1562-98; the Thirty Years War, 1618-48) in which political interests adopted a spiritual disguise.

Violence in spreading the faith can also be found at times in the field of the missions to the heathens, especially in Mexico, where in 1523 the Franciscans simply forbade the natives the worship of their gods; and in Paraguay, Uruguay, Argentina and in Portuguese Brazil, where at the beginning of the second half of the 16th century compulsory conversion and baptism were the order of the day.

In our time the temptation lies less in trying to force one's own religious ideas violently onto members of other religions than in the danger that one is blind to their spiritual values. For this reason, according to the Council, the church reminds "her sons" (where are the daughters?) "that with wisdom and love, through discussion and mutual work with those who profess other faiths—as well as through their own witness to the Christian faith and life—they must recognize, safeguard and encourage the spiritual and moral wealth and also the social and cultural worth that they find therein." (Nostra aetate, No. 2)

The insufferable intolerance that the church has displayed towards dissenters within her own ranks is almost greater than that shown towards members of other religions. We need to recall the bloody repression which was practised by the Inquisition (from the Latin *inquiere:* to investigate, to inquire into), and also its pre- and post-history. The Inquisition, contrary to a widely held view, was not a medieval invention to combat heresy. It was first raised to a papal institution by Gregory IX in 1231, and in the following year it was extended over the whole Empire by the Emperor Frederick II. But its actual origins go back into early church history. At first, only spiritual disciplinary measures (banishment from the church community) were employed against heretics, and physical force was expressly rejected (for example by Tertullian and Origen), but this had undergone a change within the Church of the Empire since Constantine. Heretics were to be punished with confiscation of property and banishment, and occasionally they were condemned to death. In the middle of the 6th century, under the Byzantine Emperor Justinian I, heresy was considered to be lèse-majéste in the sense that it was directed against the state religion, and so heretics, guilty of high treason, were burnt at the stake.

At the beginning of the 11th century this penalty was also decreed and rapidly carried through in the western world, in spite of initial protests from many theologians (among them Bernard of Clairvaux). As an enemy of the good of the community, the heretic had to be combatted by every available means. In view of the rapid spread of the Cathari and the Waldensians the Fourth Lateran Council (1215) threatened those princes who did not punish heretics with excommunication and the confiscation of their estates.

This then was the basis of the medieval Inquisition, the result of collaboration between Pope Gregory IX and the Emperor Frederick II. It obliged the state to track down heretics and those suspected of heresy. It was the task of the church to examine and judge them. The execution of judgement was delegated to the state. In itself, this Inquisition procedure was an advance in the administration of justice, in that a certain separation of powers was ensured: the state functioned as the prosecution, the church as judge. Also the inquisitional or examining procedure aimed at a fair trial.

But this separation of powers was not to last. By 1231 inquisitors appointed by the pope (mostly Dominicans and Franciscans) were also zealous in the tracking down of heretics. Innocent IV was to sanction a development of the Inquisition, as frightful in its methods as it was disastrous in its consequences; in 1252 he approved the use of torture (which was to be enforced by the secular authorities) as a means of obtaining confessions. After their conviction the "guilty" were handed over to the "secular arm." The plea lodged to spare their lives can only be understood as the expression of an indescribable cynicism or as unparalleled naiveté. For he who did not enforce the death penalty came himself under suspicion of heresy.

Although Scandinavia, England and to a lesser extent Germany, were largely spared the Inquisition, its *modus operandi* influenced their witch hunts, particularly from the middle of the 15th until the end of the 17th centuries, and also had an effect on the "reformers" who approved the persecution of heretics. In Holland and France particularly, the Inquisition claimed thousands of victims. But it was to cause the worst havoc in Spain. Pope Paul III (who also summoned the Council of Trent) had to choose Spain, of all nations, as his model when he revived the Inquisition and placed it under a College of Cardinals, the future "Sanctum Officium Sanctissimae Inquisitionis" — an authority that now bears the harmless title of the Congregation of the Holy Office. The practice of the Inquisition was abolished in southern European countries in the first half of the 19th century (Spain and Portugal) and finally, in 1870, in the Papal States.

But the spirit of the Inquisition was to remain effective within the Church for much longer, in the sense that during the course of the religious crisis at the beginning of this century which has entered history under the term of Modernism, numerous theologians were not only condemned, but also punished by disciplinary measures without being given the chance to defend themselves or to have their petitions, which were in fact justified, taken up positively. Something similar was repeated at the beginning of the fifties with some representatives of the "Nouvelle Théologie" (H. de Lubac, M.D. Chenue, Y. Congar).

It should be remembered that according to the valid order of procedure today, (Nova agendi ratio, 1971)[8], the Congregation of the Holy Office still has many arbitrary means at its disposal if it wishes to take action against an author. It is free to enforce an "extraordinary procedure" (No. 1) against him, by which the defendant only has one chance to retract — and to take note of and take upon himself the ensuing disciplinary measures. Even the "order of procedure" (which is described as a "dialogue," but whose consequences come near to that of a trial) grants the defendant no adequate protection, in that he is not entitled to the right to see the files, nor to seek the counsel of a specialist of his own choice during this "dialogue." Appeal to a higher authority is also impossible (which must give rise to the thought that the Congregation of the Holy Office considers itself to be infallible), and so is a distribution of the functions of power: the charge, examination and judgement are each and all the business of the Congregation of the Holy Office. In the secular realm of civil rights, the word prejudice would be raised in describing such conditions. It seems that the Inquisition has had long lasting consequences reaching into our most recent history and indeed, into the present.

Looking back over the past, one must bear in mind that the history of heresy is also the history of the church's blindness towards the signs of the time, and so also the history of those truths about which the church has so cautiously remained silent, as a result of a somewhat one-sided interpretation of the text on the innocence of doves and the wisdom of serpents (Mt 10.16), which were then brought up for discussion by the heretics, mostly in a one-sided and therefore distorted way. This fact should have led to an analysis of heresy, even if it had been in the form of an examination of conscience. Does not the Second Vatican Council teach that the Church, as the people of God, is at the mercy of sin during this earthly pilgrimage and therefore in constant need of renewal and conversion? (Unitatis redintegratio, No. 6). Also in its clarification of religious freedom the Council has expressly admitted the burden of guilt which the Church has placed herself under in her confrontation with dissenters: "It is certain that from time to time during the life of God's people on their pilgrimage — through the changes of human history — a manner of behavior has occured which corresponds little to the spirit of the gospel, has even been in opposition to it; but the teaching of the Church, that no one may be forced to believe, has nevertheless survived the times" (Dignitatis humanae, No. 12).

According to the Council, this "teaching constantly propagated by the (church) fathers is contained in God's word" (No. 10). According to the Gospel of St John, the free decision is left to the discretion of the individual to "take offense" (Jn 6.66, 71), and to turn away from him (Jn 6.66, 71)[9] — even if it be that one betrays him (Jn 13.27).

Just as one may not force anyone to the faith, according to the New Testament, one may also not hinder anyone from living according to his conscience. This is expressed in the answer which Peter and the apostles give to the council as a reply to their accusations. "We must obey God rather than men" (Acts 5.29). Paul also teaches the same when he refers to the Jewish diet regulations and emphasizes that everything that is done against conviction is a sin, and everything that stems from honest conviction is pleasing to God (Rom 14.23ff).

We have already pointed out that the Church, at least theoretically, was always aware of these things. Then how can it be explained that in practice this knowledge has often not been applied? The influence of St Augustine should not be underestimated. With many other church fathers[10] he held the view that no one should be forcibly converted. But later in the struggle with the Donatists (followers of a special Church in the 4th century in North Africa named after Bishop Donatus of Carthage who demanded a strict church discipline) he abandoned this belief. In his "Retractions" he explains that he had rejected compulsory measures against the heretics out of pure ignorance of their misdeeds. He based his change of view on a biblical foundation, Lk 14.23; "Compel people to come in" (those invited to supper) and he did at least rule out the death sentence for heretics. As Bishop of Carthage he represented an indisputable authority for medieval theologians, and his intolerant attitude contributed greatly to the contemporary legislation against heretics.

Simultaneously the Church's use of force against dissenters was the result of a belief rarely contested up to modern times, according to which spiritual values as such, that is, independent of the human beings who hold them, are founded in truth. Therefore it stands to reason that truth has every right to exist, whereas error has none. This implies that truth must be defended, error contested by every means available. The consequences that emerge from this for religious freedom are quite clear: he alone who professes the true faith, that is, the Catholic faith, has the right to practise his faith. What happens then, when someone is convinced *in his conscience* that he must uphold another religion?

Thomas Aquinas made some basic considerations on this point in his short work "De veritate."[11] According to him, an individual is in duty bound to a sure conscience, even when he errs in good faith. Therefore he who follows his erring conscience does it with the desire to fulfill God's Will. Whatever is done against this desire is a sin, and therefore, the erring conscience must also be respected.[12]

How can one unite this hypothesis to the former, according to which error has absolutely no right to exist? Here Thomas is confronted with the problem of religious freedom. "May one tolerate the religion of the infidels?" (*infideles:* here he means the Jews and the heathens).[13] Thomas resolves the question with the help of the theory of the weighing up of goods. One may condone a little evil in order to prevent great evil. A secular authority may therefore tolerate a certain evil, in order to avoid a great evil. For example, a state may tolerate some injustices from another state in order to avoid a disastrous war. On this point Thomas even has the New Testament on his side. In the parable of the weeds and the wheat (see Mt 13.24-30) Jesus reveals that God himself tolerates evil because through rooting it out, a greater good would be endangered. The goodness, which according to Thomas must be protected as far as the Jews are concerned, is the honor that the same God granted to them as to the Christians. Concerning the heathens, he remarks that some of them can be converted to the true faith in the course of time. In passing, it should be mentioned that this belief of Thomas's had scarcely any lasting influence on the Church's legal practices (the persecution of dissenters over the centuries).

Upon these assumptions—the sole right to the truth and consequently the exclusivity of the one true faith, a reluctant tolerance of error and so of non-Catholic confessions and non-christian religions in order to avoid greater evil—rests the pre-conciliar teaching of the Church on religious freedom, as it was presented by Leo XIII in his encyclical "Immortale Dei" of 1855.[14] The Pope was of the opinion that the true religion represented an indispensable element in public welfare. But conscience cannot benefit from error. Amongst other things, it is the duty of the state to protect and encourage the public welfare and therefore the true religion, and to prevent, if possible, the spread of other religions, as error has a damaging effect upon public welfare. A practical consequence of this opinion is that if the majority of a state is

Catholic, so must the state be "Catholic." This implies that one disputes the right of followers of another religion to profess their faith openly. If need be, one concedes that other confessions should be tolerated for the sake of public peace, that is, for a higher good. But in the case of a non-Catholic majority in a state, the Catholic minority, that is, the Church, must be granted complete freedom for the public profession of its religion.

From a contemporary viewpoint, this is certainly a distasteful outlook. But if we take the assumptions of thought into account which brought about this outlook, we cannot maintain that they are *only* an expression of arrogance and intolerance—although we would be within our rights to ask whether the Catholic Church could not have achieved more understanding somewhat earlier. In any case it is astonishing that the Church took so long to look with favor on human rights.

The Change

The Church has officially expressed her changed attitude towards the right to religious freedom in the Council's declaration of December 7, 1965, in which, amongst other things, it is said:

"The Vatican Council declares that man has the right to religious freedom. This freedom implies that he shall be freed from every compulsion, either from individuals or from groups within society or from any human force, to act against his own conscience: nor shall he be hindered from acting according to his conscience—within the recognized limits—either in private or in public, as an individual or in relation to others. Further the Council declares that the right to religious freedom itself is in truth based upon the dignity of the human being, and can itself be discerned in the revelation of the Word of God and in reason." (Dignitatis humanae, No. 2.)

Compared to earlier teaching pronouncements, this statement definitely signifies a kind of Copernican change. It came about on the strength of a consideration which had in no way been taken into account in the working out of the "traditional" teaching. This had been developed as a choice between Alternative Truth or Error. But it had been overlooked that values do not exist independently of human beings. It is always a *human person* who represents a conviction. Every

25

human being, however, possesses fundamental human rights which are not granted to him initially by an institution of society — for example by a state or a church — but are themselves rooted within the dignity of the human being. These rights, *already in existence,* must be protected by the state, by anchoring them in its constitution as civic rights. At the same time, however, the Council makes an important definition: the individual is not entitled to religious freedom in an unlimited sense, but only "within the recognized limits." Another passage explains where these limits exist: an injustice occurs against the human being and against the order into which mankind is placed by God when anyone is denied the free practice of religion in society, *"provided that lawful public order is preserved."* (No. 3; italics are mine). In other words, the boundaries of religious freedom (as indeed of freedom of conscience) are laid down here where the well-being of other human beings is at stake. It follows from this that religious freedom does not mean that every person can himself chose his faith according to his own discretion and whim, but that everyone must act according to his conscience for which before God he is responsible.

Man has not only the right, but the absolute duty to live according to his sure conscience. *Sure conscience:* this implies personal conviction, the subjective certainty to make a decision in this way and in no other. The sure conscience is *right* when it is in agreement with the objective norm. It is *erring* when a man departs from this norm in good faith. The fact of the erring conscience is a frequent occurrence in life. Naturally then, there is an obligation to pay constant attention to the education and training of the conscience. But as long as the individual does not detect an error, the sure (and in this case erring) conscience is the only moral authority that he has to obey. For, as Thomas has already taught, obedience to one's own conscience is the only chance one has to prove one's obedience toward God.

These considerations enabled the Council to reach the conclusion that a human being may not be prevented "from acting according to his conscience, especially in the realm of religion" (No. 3). A person's sure conscience must certainly be respected — provided that the welfare of others is not endangered. From this it follows that one must also treat the concrete behavior of those who think differently with respect, and concede them the right to practise their religion publicly:

"For the essence of religion exists in its realization and practice, above all in inward, deliberate and free acts through which man

26

disposes himself directly toward God; acts of this nature can neither be commanded nor prevented by pure human force. *However the social nature of man demands that he shall outwardly express his inner acts of religion,* that he will share religious matters jointly with others and acknowledge his religion publicly." (No. 3; italics are mine).

Up to this point our explanations show that the attitude of the Church towards other religions has changed considerably during the centuries: the way leads from bitter contention to reluctant tolerance to open recognition. This move from hostile polemic to open dialogue is a proof that the Church is capable of change. It gives ground for hope that the last word has not yet been spoken, particularly about some of the affairs towards which the Church today takes a restrictive attitude.

What is generally considered valid for the relationships between religions also applies to the relationship between Christianity and Judaism and Islam: intolerant behavior provokes intolerance, the readiness for dialogue leads to dialogue. The dispute about Jesus is an impressive example of this. To the extent that Christians have made an effort to exchange opinions with Jews and Muslims they have found new access to the Man from Nazareth. We are not talking here about conversion to Christianity, but a turning towards Jesus.

2 Return of the Prodigal Son: Jesus in Judaism

"Jesus is the soul of our soul as he is the flesh of our flesh. Who then would wish to exclude him from the Jewish people. St Peter is the only Jew who has said of this son of David: 'I do not know this man.' " These sentences are taken from a letter that Max Nordau, a colleague of Theodor Herzl (1860-1904), the founder of Zionism, wrote to a Catholic priest in 1899.[1] They anticipate the growing interest which Judaism has been showing towards the man from Nazareth for some decades.

In his book "Is That Not Joseph's Son? Jesus in Present-day Judaism" which was first published in 1976, Pinchas Lapide points out that no less than 187 books in *Hebrew* have been written about Jesus since the founding of the state of Israel—these include investigations, poems, plays, monographs, dissertations and essays. Lapide adds that this number is only confined to written works "whose main subject is Jesus of Nazareth. If one wanted to include the scientific monographs which deal with Jesus in connection with other movements in Judaism, the number of writings would exceed 500. And even this figure excludes works not written in Hebrew by Israeli citizens."[2] This implies that far more books have been written by Jewish authors about Jesus in the last decades than in the past one thousand eight hundred years.[3]

Legends, Polemic, Apologetic

The oldest non-Christian Jewish texts about Jesus are to be found in the Talmud. Some of the very few sections which mention Jesus by name are quoted here.

"(Mishna.) If one finds something in his (the accused's) favor, he will be let free (i.e. a judgement can be reversed if a witness produces something in defence of the accused). If not, he goes out to be stoned, because he began this or that misdemeanor; so-

28

and-so and so-and-so are his witnesses; anyone who knows anything in his favor, come and plead for him.

(Gemara.) Abbaje said: he must also say: on such and such a day, at such and such an hour, at such and such a place; perhaps there is one who knows something and comes to show them (the first witnesses) to be false witnesses.

A herald goes before him: yes, before him, not earlier. (i.e. directly before the judgement has been carried out, possible witnesses will be asked to speak if they have something to say towards the forgiveness of the condemned). About this it is taught: on the evening before the Paschal feast (Passover) they hanged Jesus. But the herald went before him for forty days (and said): this man goes out in order to be stoned, because he has practised magic and seduced and led the people of Israel astray. Anyone who knows something in his favor, come and plead for him. But they found nothing in his favor and hanged him the evening before the Passover. Ula said: do you think then, that something might have been found to favor such a one? For he was a seducer, and the All Merciful said: nor shall you spare him, nor shall you conceal him (Deut 13.9; compare 9-11). But with Jesus the case was different because he was close to the government.

Our masters taught: Jesus had five disciples; Matai, Nakai, Nezer, Buni and Toda.'' (b Sanhedrin 43a).[4]

The historical worth of this statement is slight. Historical memory is confined to the name of Jesus, possibly to that of Matthew (Matai) and to the fact that Jesus was executed. The rest is a mixture of polemic and legend. It is stated that Jesus practised magic (performed miracles), that he seduced and led the people of Israel astray; further, that he had five disciples and was executed the evening before the Passover feast.

The tendency to apologetics is easily recognizable: before a sentence of death was carried out, a herald called for possible witnesses for the defense who could save the condemned man at the last minute. In the case of Jesus, a crier searched for witnesses for a full forty days after his condemnation, and found none. The apology is directed against the Christian reproach that Jesus's trial was so short. Meanwhile there can be no doubt about his guilt because no one came forward in his favor during this long time. Finally it is emphasized that it was not the Jews but the Roman forces of occupation that destroyed Jesus, although he "was close to the government" — this again proves his guilt conclusively.

The one or two other parts of the Talmud that are concerned with Jesus are a web of polemic, legend, apologetic and vague historical memory. It is said that Jeschua or Jeschu (Jesus) of Nazareth was the fruit of an illegitimate union between a Roman officer and Miriam (Maria), the betrothed of Joseph; he was then guilty of leading the people astray, of magic, and of deriding the wise; he interpreted the wisdom of the pharisees falsely and said of himself that he was not come in order to take something away from the Torah, nor to add something to it.[5] The Talmud manuscripts devote 15 pages of nearly 15,000 to the person of Jesus. In other words, Israel's most famous son is simply mentioned in passing.

There are at least two explanations for this. Firstly, the rabbis' accounts are from the period of the Herodian temple and are treated with extreme brevity (this temple was a renovation and an enlargement of the post-exile temple building; the work began under Herod the Elder in 19 B.C.; the temple was destroyed by the Romans in 70 A.D.). Secondly, in this time of great political unrest the Jesus movement, in comparison to others, was regarded as that of a more or less unimportant sect.

The polemical tone of these few parts of the Talmud must not be over-valued. In the first place they were not concerned with discrediting Christianity. They were more an attempt to stiffen the Jews against the repression of the Church — they were virtually without rights after the election of Constantine in the 4th century. It was not a basically anti-Christian Jewish attitude but the will to self-assertion which led to Jesus legends, apologetically and polemically colored, finding their way into the Talmud.

These legends were expanded into the "Toledot Jeschu" (the generations of Jesus), probably after the 10th century. This Jewish anti-gospel was normally read in secret during the Middle Ages, and was circulated in numerous versions. As in the Talmud (b Shabbat 104b), Jesus is regarded as the illegitimate son of Mary and the Roman soldier Pandera. He receives his religious instruction from the rabbis. Later he dedicates himself to magic. He acquires supernatural powers which he puts to the service of evil by sewing a parchment with the tetragram of the four letter Hebrew name for God (JHWH = Yahweh) into his skin. Finally he is exposed as a false prophet and hanged. After they have stolen his body, his disciples announce his resurrection. An old store of legends, full of satire and folk imagination, is evident in the "Toledot Jeschu" as the impotent rebelliousness and helpless rage of a persecuted and denigrated people.

Eminent representatives of Judaism have distanced themselves from the effects of the "Toledot Jeschu." The philosopher Moses Mendelssohn (1729-1786) called them in a letter to Lavater "a monstrosity from the time of legends," Pinchas Lapide describes them as "wicked libel." Shalom Ben-Chorin speaks of a "murky source."[6] Christians doubtless take note of such judgements with a certain satisfaction. But from a Christian view the question must be asked as to how, from the Jewish side, things could have come to such a disparagement of the person of Jesus. Their precise objective was actually not Jesus but the Church, which had suppressed the Jews and in doing so, called on the name of Jesus. The distorted image of Jesus which forms the basis of the "Toledot Jeschu" is nothing more than the reaction of a persecuted minority to the policy of hatred within the Christian majority; this hatred distorted the image of Christianity's founder until it became unrecognizable. Briefly, the "Toledot Jeschu," contrary to all outward appearances, are not the product of an "anti-Jesus" force, but the expression of an anti-Christianism provoked by the Christians themselves.

The same can be said of the rabbis of the Middle Ages, as Pinchas Lapide has suggested in an analysis which is both comprehensive and convincing. Their rejection is not of the pre-gospel Jesus, but of those who honor him as God.[7] This applies, for example, to Rabbi Salomo Ben Isaak (1040-1105) who became world-famous under the name of Raschi, and in whose bible commentary "Jeschu the Nazarene" — referring to the Talmud — Jesus was described as a rabble-rouser (b Sanhedrin 43a). However on closer inspection it turns out that Raschi projects the Christian teaching of the Trinity back onto the historical person of Jesus and therefore, in the sense of Deut 13.7-12, sees him as an instigator of apostasy and a rabble-rouser. It is not the historical Jesus, but the formulated dogma of the Trinity which is the object of attack.

Some medieval rabbis — as indeed other Jewish scholars of the time — developed an essentially positive relationship to the figure of Jesus, (this was also so in Islam), and thus made a step toward ecumenism long before the movement had any significance of its own.

31

We must not forget Moses Maimonides, whose position in Judaism was comparable to that of Thomas Aquinas in Christendom. Maimonides ranks as a universal genius of the Middle Ages, and as one of the leading figures responsible for bringing the Jews into the Diaspora. This is expressed in the famous word play; "from Moses until Moses there was no one like Moses." This "second Moses" was born in Cordoba in Spain in 1135 and died in Fostat near Cairo in 1204.

While Christians see in Jesus the completion of the Jewish Law and the fulfilment of messianic hope, in his main work "Mischne Tora" (Revision of the Law) Maimonides expresses another viewpoint: Jesus, together with Muhammad, paves the way for the messianic age expected by the Jews.

"All these matters which refer to Jesus of Nazareth and the Ismaelite (Muhammad) who came after him, only served to pave the way for the King Messiah, and to prepare the whole world for the worshipping of God with united hearts, as it is written [Zeph 3.9 follows]. In this fashion the messianic hope, the Torah and the commandments have become the most widely spread and general store of faith — amongst the inhabitants of the distant islands and among many peoples, uncircumcised in heart and flesh."[8]

The Jewish doctor and philospher Sa'd Ibn Mansur Ibn Kammuna (1215-1285) thinks as Maimonides. For him the three greatest monotheistic religions rest upon one divine revelation. He approaches the figure of Jesus with great deference and open-mindedness. There is no more talk of a magician or a rabble-rouser:

"There was no doubt about the state of death and the sicknesses of those whom Jesus brought back to life and could heal. Any doubts would have been communicated immediately to his adversaries, whether Jews or not. However, no doubts have been reported, although some of his miracles have been attributed to magic, or to the devil's help, or to calling on the name of God. But it is well established that no deception or tricks of any kind were played on Jesus's contemporaries." Jesus and his apostles were "pious Jews until the end of their lives." However there is no lack of critical allusion to the Church: "Jesus rose, washed his apostles' feet and said: the son of man is not come to be served, but to serve. Herein lies his true greatness...In the gospels it is said: if your faith were half as big as a mustard seed you could say to this mountain: 'move over there' — and it would obey. Today, however, we find no believers in Jesus who would be capable of moving a pebble."[9]

When the princes of the Church in the late Middle Ages staged public disputations with the rabbis in order to compel them to profess Christ, they achieved exactly the opposite effect: the main result was not acceptance of the Christian faith but a sharper rejection of it. Shortly after such a disputation in 1399, Rabbi Schemtov Lippmann from Mulhouse wrote his "Book of Refutation," which to some extent represented a *Summa contra christianos*. One example illustrates the kind of argumentation he used. When the Christian theologians, referring to the church fathers, cited God's decision "Let us make man" (Gen 1.26) as a proof of the Trinity because of the plural form, Rabbi Lippmann pointed out the singular form of the following verse: "So God created man" (Gen 1.27) and ironically commented that "the son had obviously been disobedient and let his father do the work alone" — and therefore the latter deserted him when he cried for help on the cross.[10]

These spectacular disputations became ever more frequent, with the result that the Jews showed a growing interest in the New Testament in order to be able to refute the Christians with arguments out of *their* sacred texts.

Approaches to Jesus

With regard to the teaching of the faith, the rise of the humanist movement and the spread of the Reformation brought about a more relaxed relationship between Christians and Jews. Some of the rabbis living in an environment hostile to Jews and under a legislation (if not of the Church) which despised them, could even contemplate the founder of Christianity with respect, sometimes with affection. An example of this is Rabbi Jakob Emden (1696-1776). In spite of a tendency to fanaticism in internal Jewish questions of faith, he showed himself to be distinctly open-minded towards the figure of Jesus and Christianity:

"The founder of Christianity has done the world a double favor. On the one hand, he consolidated Moses's Torah with all his strength, for none of our wise men has emphasized and confirmed with greater stress the eternal binding force of God's teaching. On the other hand, he did the heathens a great favor (if

33

they had only not wrecked his noble intention, as certain fatheads who were not able to grasp the true meaning of the gospel have done) in that he did away with false gods, freed them from idolatry and bound them to the seven commandments of Noah...In fact he tried to perfect them through a moral teaching which is far harder than the Torah of Moses.

The founder of Christendom never thought of dissolving the Torah. That was also the view of his disciple Paul...The disciples of the Nazarene chose those people who did not wish to join Judaism; chose the font and not circumcision; chose Sunday instead of the Sabbath as the weekly day of rest; in order to bear witness that they were not pure Jews. But the Nazarene and his apostles adhered strictly to the Sabbath and to circumcision because they were Jews from birth and descent, and observed the complete Torah...Christianity should have been founded only for the heathens."[11]

Moses Mendelssohn, a contemporary of Rabbi Emden, makes similar comments. He also emphasizes that Jesus did not break with Jewish tradition: "Jesus of Nazareth himself not only observed the law of Moses but also the rules of the rabbis; that which may appear to be contradictory in his words and deeds only seems so at first sight. On careful examination, everything is consistent with the scriptures and with their transmission."[12]

These previous summaries could easily convey the impression that the figure of Jesus has commanded a significant attention within Judaism. But this impression is deceptive. We have been concerned with isolated representatives of Judaism who have had serious thoughts about the Man from Nazareth. Jesus plays an unimportant role in the history of Jewish faith when we consider it as a whole. Usually he is passed over in silence. The fear that negative comments could result in sanctions from the state or the Church was only too well grounded. Such voices as those of Rabbi Emden or Moses Mendelssohn were the exceptions that prove the rule.

It is not to the credit of the Church that some followers of Judaism in the course of time suddenly discovered Jesus. Neither the public disputations of faith which she arranged, nor the compulsory attendance of "conversion" sermons which continued into the late 18th century, nor the persecutions and the massive social discrimination were able to bring Jesus any nearer to the Jews.

34

But a rapprochement has indeed taken place, not directly along the path of religion, but along the indirect way of the biblical criticism of numerous 19th century Protestant theologians. While some of them at first saw Jesus as an invention of the evangelists and seriously challenged his historicity, others subsequently pointed out the difference between Jesus's preaching and the faith of the early Christians. Agreement was soon reached with regard to the fact that the gospels reported more than historical events and therefore cannot be regarded as historical sources in the modern sense. These manuscripts are not concerned with bureaucratic-like records, but with testaments of faith. In other words, the evangelists interpret the figure of Jesus, they announce him as the Messiah, they proclaim him as the Son of God. Not only the preaching and practice of Jesus are present in the gospels, but also faith in Jesus as the Messiah and Redeemer. Realizing this, Christian theology saw itself faced with the necessity of furnishing proof that this faith (as it was later formulated in the dogmas) represented the legitimate exposition of Jesus's aims and was in harmony with his sense of mission. In short, it was necessary to demonstrate in what way the proclamation of Jesus constrasted with the teaching of the rabbis of his time and with the tradition of Judaism.

It was natural that the interest of Jews tended in the opposite direction. They too wanted to get behind church dogmas — but instead of finding the exposition of Jesus's teaching in them, they came upon later "painted-over" versions of his figure which had then to be removed, layer by layer, in order to find Jesus himself. Behind the Messiah proclaimed by the Church they had to find the proclaimer Jesus; behind the Son of God, the Son of Man; behind the Christ of belief, the believing Jew. While Christian theology emphasized the extent to which Jesus differed from the Judaism of his time, the Jewish researchers underlined those features which bound him to his contemporaries.

Both Rabbi Emden and Moses Mendelssohn were of the opinion that Jesus adapted himself to the Judaism of the time, and that his message must be explained from this point of view. One of the first rabbis to argue this thesis systematically was Samuel Hirsch (1808-1889), who became President of the Reform Rabbinical Assembly of the United States in 1869. In his work "The System of Jewish Religious Opinion and its Relationship to Heathendom, Christianity and to Absolute Religion" (Frankfurt/Main, 1842), Hirsch holds that everything concerning the teaching of Judaism in the gospels and especially in

Paul, has nothing to do with Jesus's thought, but is a later addition of the (pagan-christian) Church. Hirsch sees Jesus as a most exemplary Jew, who lives out his faith completely and fully. That he erred in respect of the actual imminent divine ascendancy does not detract from his greatness; on the contrary, this error is the result and expression of the primal Jewish longing for messianic salvation.

Samuel Hirsch's attitude signalled a change in the Jewish assessment of Jesus which took place around the middle of the last century. Research on the Man from Nazareth grew and, with a few exceptions, it was positive.[13]

Rabbi H. G. Enelow (1877-1934) speaks for many others: "Amongst all that is good and great that humanity has produced, nothing comes so near the universal as the claims and authority of Jesus. He has become the most charismatic figure in world history. Within his person the best and the deepest of Israel, of the eternal people whose son he was, are united...The Jew cannot avoid being proud of what Jesus means for the world. Nor can he dismiss the hope that Jesus will become the link of union between Jew and Christian, after which misunderstandings will be put aside and his teaching really understood."[14]

Why then, has the figure of Jesus commanded so little attention in the history of Judaism over the centuries? Rabbi Enelow has an explanation: it is the fault of the Church and it is an invitation to examination of conscience: "When we consider the diversity of the teachings, systems, regimes, cults and doctrines that have all been legitimized and sanctioned in the name of Jesus, how much inhumanity has been done in his name, how he has been used as an excuse for Jewish suffering and the murder of countless Jews, then we can understand why so little attention has been paid to him during the course of Jewish history."[15]

Jesus — A "Jew Among Jews"

Judaism's new discovery of Jesus led to a detailed study of him and his teachings by numerous Jewish scholars. The first book in Hebrew about him in recent times was written in 1922 by Joseph Klausner, a historian at the Hebrew University in Jerusalem.[16] Klausner sees Jesus as the most Jewish of Jews. His preaching is in complete harmony with that of

36

Moses and the prophets, although it must be said that he sets far too high a standard, and therefore demands too much of mankind. His ethic may well be ideal for individuals and so, to a certain extent, represents an example for the world to come. In contrast, Jewish ethic is designed for this world, to be realized within it. For this reason Jesus's teaching has never been accepted by Israel. According to Klausner, there is no doubt that Jesus was convinced of his messianism. But as the Messiah, he is only the tool of redemption through Yahweh and in no sense himself a redeemer-god. Klausner summarizes his judgement of Jesus in the last chapter of his book:

"His moral teaching is sublime, more refined and original in its form than any other Hebrew ethical system. His wonderful similes are without comparison. The keen perception, the brevity of his sayings and the effectiveness of his parables, mean that to an extraordinary extent his ideas are the property of us all. And if the day comes when this ethic can shed its mystical and miraculous overlay, then Jesus's book of ethics will be one of the most precious treasures in Jewish literature of all time."[17]

The last great rabbi of the Jewish community in Berlin, Leo Baeck (1873-1956) thinks along the same lines as Klausner. He understood and interpreted "The Gospel as a Document of the History of Jewish Faith" (the title of one of his most important works). According to Baeck, the original gospel tradition contains "nothing other than every tradition in the Jewish world of those days."[18] The gospel "is a Jewish book...for the pure air which fills it and in which it breathes is that of the sacred scriptures, because the Jewish spirit and only the Jewish spirit prevails over it. It is entirely pervaded by Jewish belief and Jewish hope, Jewish suffering and Jewish affliction, Jewish knowledge and Jewish expectation—it is a Jewish book among Jewish books."[19]

If Jesus—as many others—understood himself as the Messiah, it does not mean, Baeck suggests, that he *is* the Messiah but only that he wanted to bring about the kingdom of God, which is still not here:

"In the old gospel that reveals itself in this way, a man with noble features stands before us, who lived and helped and worked, endured and died in the country of the Jews during agitated and tense times, a man of the Jewish people, of Jewish ways, of Jewish faith and hope, whose spirit lived in the holy scripture, who spoke poetry in it and

37

meditated in it, and who proclaimed and taught the word of God because it was given to him from God to listen and to preach. Before us stands a man who had won his disciples from among his people, they who were looking for the Messiah, the son of David, the promised one, and then found him and held fast to him, believed in him until he began to believe in himself, so that he entered into the mission and the destiny of his times, and into the history of mankind. These disciples were possessed by him and they believed in him beyond his death, so that it became a certainty in their lives that, as the prophet had foretold, he would 'rise again from the dead on the third day.' The man we see before us in these old records demonstrates the stamp of everything Jewish in every line and feature of his being, reveals in them so typically and so clearly what is pure and good in Judaism; a man who, as he was, could only have grown out of this soil of Judaism, and could only have acquired his disciples and followers as they were, from this same soil. A man who here alone in this Jewish sphere, in Jewish trust and yearning, could go through his life and his death — a Jew among Jews."[20]

Martin Buber (1878-1965), the Jewish religious philosopher, expressed himself in a similar fashion. For him, Jesus's message is Jewish through and through; as in the Old Testament and in Judaism itself, Jesus proclaims the Kingdom (Realm) of God, faith, and return to God. Thanks to Jesus's closeness to his own faith, Buber is able to profess himself to Jesus as to "my great brother":

"My own brotherly receptive relationship to him has become stronger and purer, and I see him today with a stronger and purer gaze than ever before. I am also now more certain that a great position will be granted to him in the history of the Jewish faith, and that this position cannot be fitted into any of the usual categories...that Christianity has seen and still continues to see him as God seems to me to be a fact of the greatest seriousness, which I must seek to comprehend, both for his and my sake..."[21]

Buber here expresses what Shalom Ben-Chorin (1913-), one of the leading champions of a better understanding between Jews and Christians, formulated in his book "Brother Jesus: The Nazarene from a Jewish View" (first published in 1967). He says: "Jesus's belief unites us, belief *in* Jesus divides us."[22] On the one hand Ben-Chorin's book is a passionate profession of Jesus, the Jewish brother; on the other hand it presents a decisive negation of the Christian Kyrios and Messiah. After admitting to this the author makes an effort to familiarize himself with the gospel, the ground roots of Christianity, and in doing so he "stumbles upon a precious part of his own land" (191). Jesus can be compared to the prodigal son in the parable:

"He himself, the teller of this parable, becomes, clearly against his own will, 'Israel's Prodigal Son.' For almost two thousand years he has lingered in a foreign land, while the elder brother—the Jewish people—has remained under the strict control of the Father. Now, though, it seems that the process of his return to the Jewish people has begun" (81).

"Jesus of Nazareth lived—he lives on, not only in his Church which uses his name (it would be more realistic to say in the many churches and sects which have a claim on him), but also in his people whose martyrdom he embodies. Has not the suffering and ridiculed Jesus, dying on the cross, become a parable for his whole people who, bloodily castigated, has hung again and again on the cross of hatred for the Jews?"(24)

For Ben-Chorin Jesus is active along the lines of the teachers of the Law of his time, which mostly links him to the Pharisees, although he cannot really be fitted into any Jewish party or religious movement. Ben-Chorin takes his healing of the sick extremely seriously, as the outcome of a suggested power (50). Closely associated with this is his work as a teacher, which Jesus certainly carried out with "a greater power of authority than others would have risked" (14) and which led away from a dispensible faith towards an "intensifying of the Law, in which love formed the decisive, dynamic element" (15). Jesus "was neither a dogmatist nor a systematist, for he was—a Jew. He spoke and acted out of the situation, and the unconditional quality of individual statements caused violence to be done to him" (63).

Ben-Chorin constantly emphasizes that Jesus is rooted in Jewish tradition. In the Sermon on the Mount he finds a "piece from the store of Jewish teaching which fits organically into the tradition of rabbinical Judaism, even if certain individual features of the preacher are visible" (55). This also applies to the parables: ("Jesus, who was completely and utterly a Jew in the tradition of his Jewish fatherland, here too remains within his tradition" 75); to the prayer that he teaches his disciples ("a Jewish prayer from the first to the last word" 91); to his sermon on the Kingdom of God ("the heart of the prophetic message" 125).

For Ben-Chorin even the Seder ceremony (the Lord's Supper) is "not something entirely new but a renewal of ancient tradition" (128). In this connection he asumes "that Jesus did not think of himself as the Messiah" — but this does not rule out "that he certainly felt himself ready to sacrifice his life. That this sacrifice then received a messianic stamp could have been the result of a later and broader interpretation of the events" (130). In the meantime Jesus wanted "to add to this meal in memory of the Exodus from Egypt, the memory of his own sacrifice" (140). But Jesus was not able to bring about the Kingdom of God through this "freely chosen sacrifice of his life" — and therefore "from a Jewish-historical view he went tragically astray, and his eyes were blinded by his love of Israel," which however does not "diminish his greatness in the least" (23). For Ben-Chorin, that Jesus erred springs from the fact that the redemption in which Christians believe is in no sense tangible: "We await the absolute redemption...and know of no redemptive enclaves in the midst of an unredeemed world."[23]

Ben-Chorin sees Jesus as an exemplary Jew — and only a Jew. Christians see in him the elevated Kyrios and Christ. According to Ben-Chorin "with him, we have nothing to do" (188). "The Hellenistic Diaspora-Judaism made its first conclusive appearance with Paul, in the forming of the Kerygmas, the proclamation of Christian faith." But "Jesus and his disciples were Jews. Out and out Jews, and only Jews" (189).

Also Jesus is an exemplary human being — and only a human being. He reveals his whole humanity particularly in the Garden of Gethsemane. "Here a human being trembles for his life. And in this hour of fear Jesus is especially close to us. I find it incomprehensible that one can understand this human tragedy against the background of a dogma of the double nature of Christ: true man and true God" (148). It would never have occurred to Jesus himself to "ask the disciples to worship him" (92). Even when "now and again an intimation of a messianic calling as an unanswered question of his existence may have broken out in Jesus, the question of his divinity cannot exist for the historian or for the Jew" (13).

Understandably for Ben-Chorin, Jesus' destiny ends with his death. On the other hand "the history of Jesus" (186) begins with the

40

discovery of the empty tomb. Ben-Chorin argues strictly historically. For this reason alone it is astonishing that he does not consider the disciples' belief in Easter—which, in contrast to Jesus's resurrection, is historically tangible—worthy of any further analysis. According to Jewish understanding, Jesus failed (23) and as a result of his death on the cross is regarded as cursed by God (Deut 21.23: "for a hanged man is accursed by God"); inevitably the question must be asked how his disciples, also Jews (189), succeeded in proclaiming such a man as savior of the world and redeemer of mankind.

Pinchas Lapide (1922-   ),[24] like Shalom Ben-Chorin, sees Jesus as an embodiment of Israel and its destiny:

"For Jews—who were always persecuted, who were always the first victims of man's injustice and inhumanity in the history of the world, who all too often have had to carry the cross in which Christians believe,—in spite of all the power and all the force in the holy relics, could claim that you can find no better embodiment of this Jewish people than in this poor Rabbi from Nazareth. *Eli, Eli lama sabachtani* is not only David's psalm and Jesus's words from the cross, but, I would go so far as to say, it is the leitmotif of those who had to go to Auschwitz and Maidanek" (Conflict, 17).

Lapide points out that Jesus's sermons and his practice are totally and completely anchored in the Judaism of the time:

"The Our Father amounts to an abridged version of the synagogue liturgy; the whole of the Sermon on the Mount, together with loving your enemies, is built up out of rabbinical components, and together with all Jesus's parables only reveals its full meaning against its Jewish background" (Salvation, 60).

Jesus is absolutely "true to the Torah"; never and nowhere did he "break the law of Moses or in any way demand its infringement" (Conflict, 25, 26). In fact—like other contemporary rabbis—he "reinterpreted some rules." This only "makes him more rabbinical" (ibid 34).

"In relation to the Judaism of his time, Jesus stood in contrast and in harmony; for me, both these words make him Jewish through and through—I would almost go so far as to say only Jewish. How? We can establish that his spirit was Jewish in at least six ways: in his hope, in his eschatology, in his Jewish ethos, in his blind trust in God, in his good-Jewish messianic impatience, and last but not least, in his Jewish suffering. This is clear from all the four gospels. That he often stood in opposition to the world around him also makes him Jewish, because I do

41

not know of any Jewish luminary, from Moses on, who did not arouse lively resistance among the Jewish people. We have no greater Jew than Moses. Read in the Book of Exodus how these Jewish people put their leader out of countenance six times, were nearly always mutinous towards him, and twice in the desert it came to rebellions that almost cost him his life. The same can be said for a dozen other great Jews who years later, centuries after their deaths, were pronounced "holy" (canonized, as you would say in your Church). That Jesus formed a contrast, that he had enemies and opposers, is one of the most striking proofs of his greatness, not of his un-Jewishness" (Conflict, 23ff).

Lapide has nothing against Christians also calling upon Jesus: "But then they must think of themselves as 'those who have come along,' as 'those included'; or as Paul calls them (Eph 2.19; 3.6) 'fellow-citizens, fellow-heirs, members of the same body, and partakers of the promise,' but not as successors, usurpers, expropriators, even 'inheritors' of a still vibrant Israel. According to Duden, one can only inherit from someone's estate when they are dead" (Salvation, 65).

The person of Jesus poses an open-ended question for Jews as to "whether his workings in their pious God-fearing Jewishness have exhausted themselves. In other words: was he nothing more than an itinerant teacher, pharisee and speaker of parables?" (Jews and Christians, 65). Finally, Lapide refrains from answering this clearly. In one sense the Nazarene is only a man for him — but in a most exemplary way:

"I have occupied myself with him for the past thirty years, with his teaching and the history of his activities; but many enigmas remain unanswered; several of his features are indistinct for me, and his exact identity eludes all research...If the conversion of mankind to the God of Israel is the penultimate goal of world history, then the christianizing of a billion human beings which happened in the name of Jesus is an important step forwards along this way of salvation. I have to admit that I cannot acknowledge Jesus either as Israel's Messiah or as the redeemer of an unredeemed world; but that God used him in order to bring about a forward movement, an advance along the way of redemption, is a fact of profound theological magnitude. Also I cannot accept his birth as the incarnation of God — in the Christian sense of the word — but his exemplary humanity as 'vere homo,' which has much to say to us and which can help us towards a deeper, nobler humanity, all this is and remains the basis for futher discussions" (Salvation, 92ff).

42

But on the other hand, the fact that Jesus could be the Messiah cannot be completely excluded from the Jewish view: "Christians believe he is the savior of the world; Jews say, for us he is not Israel's Messiah—or at least not yet" (ibid. 107). Lapide was to formulate the concrete meaning of this in a long dialogue with Karl Rahner:

"The Church prays daily for the Parusie Christi, the Synagogue for the coming of the Messiah. In Christian soteriology and in Jewish messianic teaching there can only be one, universal bringer of salvation; so it follows that he who is so ardently awaited must be our mutual redeemer. For you it is certain that he will be Jesus of Nazareth; for me this is a possibility that cannot entirely be ruled out. No more, but no less. There is not a Jewish No against a Christian Yes, but a Christian Yes against a humble Jewish question mark" (Salvation, 88ff).

For Christians, Jesus's resurrection represents a confirmation that Jesus is the promised savior. In Judaism however, the thought of resurrection is not bound up with the expectation of messianic salvation (Resurrection, 93); so that not until eschatological fulfilment will it be proved whether Jesus is the Messiah or not. Until then, the question still exists for Lapide. But he has made the greatest possible approach to Christianity that can be achieved by a follower of Judaism, without giving up his faith in the process. That he cannot do, however, so long as the history of mankind seems to refute the Christian belief in the redeemer, and rather to agree with the Jews who are still waiting for the messianic redemption (see Salvation, 79ff).

David Flusser, Professor of New Testament Studies in Jerusalem, also approaches the figure of Jesus with great knowledge and sensitivity.[25] While Ben-Chorin prefers to consult St John's gospel in his book about Jesus, Flusser's is based mainly on the synoptics, so it is clear that for him too, Jesus can only be understood within his Jewish milieu. For Flusser, as for Ben-Chorin, the radical ethic of love forms the real reason as to why Jesus provoked the opposition of the authorities of the time—although in this respect the behavior of Jesus emphatically does not represent a break with Jewish tradition; on the contrary, it can only be explained because of it: "one could easily assemble a whole gospel from the old Jewish scriptures without a word of it having to originate from Jesus." But Flusser also concedes that one "could only do this because we actually possess the gospels" (70). However, one has to allow Jesus a certain uniqueness, because it is a fact that he is "the only known Jew from antiquity who not only proclaimed that we were on the edge of the end of time, but simultaneously that the new time millenium had begun" (87).

Flusser depicts Jesus as a law-abiding Jew, but he does not rule out the fact that Jesus himself, during the course of an inner development, understood himself to be the Son of Man in the sense of the Redeemer—and possibly even to be the Messiah—but in that respect he was mistaken regarding the carrying out of his mission. However the person of Jesus has a right to a significance in the history of salvation, in so far as in an exemplary fashion he revealed to mankind the way to become a fulfilled human being. None of the intrepretations of Jesus from Joseph Klausner, Leo Baeck, Martin Buber, Shalom Ben-Chorin, Pinchas Lapide and David Flusser go beyond that boundary represented by the Church's dogma of Jesus as God and Man. The Jewish intrepretations of Jesus are not interested in 'vere Deus' (Jesus as the true God). Or, better expressed, they are interested in it only in so far as they must reject it. But for a deeper understanding of 'vere homo' (the true Man) they are able, as Heinrich Fries remarks, to contribute a great deal to what touches not only "the man but the Jew Jesus, his faith, his message of God's sovereignty and kingdom...The problems of Law and Gospel, Law and Grace, and the redemption not yet accomplished become alive in a new way."[26]

The emphasis on Jesus's closeness to Judaism makes it particularly clear that the Old Testament represents a key to an understanding of New Testament literature. It is understandable that the Christian will decline to agree with the thesis which sees Jesus only as the Prodigal Son who finally returns home to his Father's house after nearly two thousand years. That the bringing home (to put it more correctly) has only been forthcoming after such a long time is also the fault of the Church, which has so frequently hidden the sight of Jesus from Judaism. The Second Vatican Council admits this implicitly—although one could ask whether the admission of fault could not have been a little more noticeable.[27]

The bringing home of Jesus, not only to his father's house but also to his fatherland has in the meantime occurred at another level. After no or hardly any mention of him in Jewish writings over the centuries because of Jewish legislation or through fear of the Church's measures of punishment, new Israeli school books are dealing with him, sometimes in great detail. Ten Israeli history books that were in use in Israel between 1946 and 1971 have been analysed by Pinchas Lapide for what they have to say about Jesus's origins, John the Baptist, Jesus's message, his messianic claim, about his judgement and crucifixion and also about the gospels and early Christianity.[28] He summarizes the result:

> "1.   Jesus is never burdened with the later Christian guilt of hatred toward the Jews, neither are conclusions about the Church drawn to the disadvantage of the Nazarene.
>
> 2.   However, the Jewishness of Jesus, which is taken for granted by all the texts, leads to various interpretations of his historical role—contender for the Messiahship, proclaimer of the end of time, political agitator, moral preacher or a patriotic rebel against the yoke of the heathens—but the result is an unambiguous, more or less emphatic identification with the Nazarene when the subject is his martyr's death on the cross of the Romans.
>
> 3.   Although some of the texts speak of Jesus's 'deviation' from the normative Judaism of his time, they are far outweighed by the references to his 'faithfulness to the Torah,' his ties to the Bible and his Jewish ethos...."

With the single exception of the gospels or their sources, which have been described correctly as documents of Jewish faith, the contemporary school books in Israel without any doubt comprise the most sympathetic image of Jesus offered to any generation of Jewish children by their teachers." (78ff.)

Lapide concludes his analysis by asking a question: "Could not the Jewish image of Jesus in today's teaching serve as a model of tolerance in order to give the image of Judaism in Christian teaching a more truly Christian form?" (80).

During the last decades some Jewish novelists have concerned themselves with the figure of Jesus. I would first like to mention those historical and psychological Jesus novels from the forties to the sixties which aroused the historical interest and archeological curiosity of readers of that time, as well as appeasing their hunger for metaphysics.

Of this genre the novel "Der man fun Notzers" (1939: German ed. "The Nazarene," 1957, new ed. "Jesus. The Nazarene," Zurich 1987) by Sholom Asch (1880-1957) was widely read and hotly debated. Asch makes use of indirect portrayal. From the confrontation between Jochanan, a pupil of Nicodemus (the author's narrator in the first-person) and Pan Viadomsky, a former army captain from Jerusalem, an image of Jesus emerges which seems perfectly orthodox to the Christian reader. Jesus is condemned to death by an unlawful procedure because he has aspired towards a renewal of Jewish faith. Asch was fiercely attacked for this novel by orthodox Jews, especially those coming from Eastern Europe. He was accused of interceding for Christianity, thus supporting heresy and motivating his readers to convert.

"Der Meister" — "The Master" (1952) by Max Brod (1884-1968) could also have been written by a Christian. Here and there Brod also employs indirect portrayal, but to a certain extent he stands above his characters and describes Jesus from the viewpoint of the all-knowing narrator. Jeshua (Jesus), the protagonist, is accompanied by three other characters who make it possible for the narrator to portray him from various perspectives. There is Meleagros the Greek, a cool-headed intellectual, who is Pontius Pilate's secretary and lives in Jerusalem. There he comes across Jehuda (Judas) his earlier student friend and a nihilist who has joined the Master because he sees in him a prophet of doom who will lead the world towards its end. The third main character with the Master is his half-sister Schoschana, who is unable to reciprocate Meleagros's love. She awaits the Kingdom of God, which her half-brother proclaims. But this proclamation is misunderstood by the Master's followers as a call to rebellion against the Romans. Jesus is finally betrayed, arrested, condemned. Schoschana suffers death when she tries to rescue her brother on the path to Golgotha. Meleagros retires to Galilee and joins the Master's followers. In this novel Jesus appears as a Jewish prophet within the framework of tradition. The question of his messianism is presented less from the author's point of view than from the views of his characters—and these answer it in very different ways. This means that neither Christian nor Jewish readers will be offended.

The novel "Bamich'ol hazar" ("The Narrow Path" 1938: English tr. Tel Aviv, 1968) by Ahron Abraham Kabak (1880-1944) counts as "one of the most convincing portrayals of the Jewish Master from Galilee."[29] Kabak portrays a Jesus who is firmly rooted in his people and will acquire salvation for them and for all mankind. His sermons are so evocative of the Old Testament that he can himself be ranked among the prophets. His whole proclamation aims at awakening and consolidating faith in the living God. The author expresses this clearly at the end of the dialogue between Jesus and Nicodemus, which takes place a few hours before Jesus's arrest and also forms the end of the novel:

> "Nakidom, my brother! There is no death in the world! There is only a passing from one life to another....If all people in all countries would no longer believe in death and fasten their belief onto the living God, who reigns in them and outside them, in the cross there, and in the crucified—but also in the crucifiers—then Nakidom, ah then..."[30]

The Jewish novelist Frank Andermann (1909-) rails against both Jews and Christians in his novel "Das große Gesicht" "The Great Face" (Munich 1970) which is partly based on autobiographical occurrences. The first-person narrator Alfred Rubin, a Jew by birth, projects the experience of being persecuted onto the persecuted Jew Jesus. His own fate as a Jewish resistance fighter at the time of National Socialism leads him to see Jesus as the protagonist of the Jewish resistance. Therefore, in Rudin's reconstruction of events, all had to be omitted "that was not the bare facts of life, everything miraculous, mysterious, everything theologically veiled and fabricated for reasons of faith, the complete legend of the itinerant preacher and miracle-worker" (103 ff). What is left is a figure who develops from a thirty-year-old provincial into a decisive partisan, and who never thought of resurrection (which was invented by the apostles) but only of rebellion. He appoints Peter and Judas to betray him so that attention will be drawn away from the Galilean resistance group and the common cause can be saved. Here Andermann takes up a hypothesis which had already been supported by

Joel Carmichael ("The Death of Jesus" New York, 1963), and Robert Eisler ("Jesus basileus ou basileusas. Die messianische Unabhängigkeitsbewegung vom Auftreten Johannes des Täufers bis zum Untergang Jakobs des Gerechten" Heidelberg, 1929/30; "Jesus Basileus ou basileusas. The messianic independence movement from the appearance of John the Baptist to the decline of Jacob the Just"). These authors convincingly reject the accusation that Jesus was made into a "wretched figure" (88) by his followers. But representatives of the Jewish faith cannot welcome Andermann's attempt to win Jesus back for Judaism. His Jesus is a man without belief.

One also comes across traces of Jesus in some of the best known poetry of contemporary Jewish poets. Nelly Sachs (1981-1970) comes to mind: "Immer noch Mitternacht" ("Still Midnight"); "Dornengekrönt" ("Crowned with Thorns"); "David". And Paul Celan (1920-1970): "Tenebrae"; "Psalm"; "Mandorla." Also Hilde Domin (1912-) whose short but comprehensive poem "Ecce Homo" is representative of contemporary Jewish poetry about Jesus:

> Less than the hope in him
> that is human kind
> one-armed
> always
>
> Only the crucified one
> both arms
> wide open
> the Here-I-am[31]

Results, Questions, Consequences

A combination of some results, questions and consequences can be registered. We can ascertain that Jewish interest in Jesus has been reawakened during the last decades, and that, seen as a whole, there is no polemical intention behind this interest. Jewish religious philosophers, scholars and literati have granted Jesus right of domicile again, after his expatriation from Judaism over the centuries. They even see him as a guiding light in Judaism. But this only applies to some important advocates of Judaism. Some of these (including Ben-Chorin and Pinchas Lapide) point to the fact that the destiny of the Jewish people is reflected in the fate of Jesus. He becomes a prototype of the persecuted Jews, his passion a symbol of the suffering of his people. The Jewish painter Marc Chagall has expressed this most movingly in his "White Crucifixion" (1938): surrounded by dead Jews, destroyed houses, burning synagogues and scorched Torah rolls, Jesus hangs on the cross dressed in the tallit, the Jewish mantle of prayer.

Present Jewish interest in Jesus is directed towards what he taught and how he lived, not towards who he is, according to Christian understanding. Concerning this the exegete Franz Mußner has raised a question which has never been seriously discussed in Christian theology, even though it is of the greatest importance in Jewish-Christian dialogue — "Was Jesus of Nazareth recognizable to Israel in accordance with later christological dogmas?"[32] Mußner points out that the "obscure origins of Jesus" have already played a role that should not be underestimated in the discussions about his mission (313), because Israel "could not reconcile his origin with his claim" (320), and that "in one of the harshest scenes which Mark knew from the oldest Jesus material" (314), even Jesus's followers were convinced that he must be "beside himself" — that is, mad (Mk 3.20 ff). But if, Mußner asks, the messianic-divine mission of Jesus was hidden, even from his nearest relatives "how then should the whole of Israel recognize him?" (315). This question is all the more justifiable when one considers that the later church profession of Christ goes back to the development within how Jesus saw himself and not to the contemporary Jewish conception of the Messiah. To put it differently, most of Jesus's contemporaries and fellow-believers were unable to identify him with the Messiah because they had completely different expectations of this concept. "The christian 'Dogma' that the crucified Jesus is the promised Messiah is particularly 'scandalous' for the Jews and will remain so (1 Cor 1.23). The Christian must understand this." (317) There is no need to be silent here about the reproach against the obstinacy of Israel which comes from Paul (Rom 11.28-32). But Paul simply took the disobedience of Israel as a fact, without questioning the reasons and the background. "We are not talking about a proof of guilt" (331). Paul's argument is neither anthropological nor psychological but purely theological: the ways that God's design for salvation still achieve their goal are unfathomable! (see Rom 11.32 ff).

Certainly there are Jews who have turned towards Christianity. Well known examples include the Chief Rabbi of Rome, Italo Zolli (Israel Zoller) who was baptized on the 13 February 1945 with the name of his honorary godfather Eugenio (Pacelli—Pius XII); Edith Stein, who found her way to the Catholic faith by reading the autobiography of St Teresa of Avila; the philosopher Simone Weil, who however would not be baptized out of solidarity with those who did not find their way to the Church.

The fact that such conversions are the exception rather than the rule is doubtless linked to the professing of Christ based on the New Testament (true God from true God, one with the Father; mediator between God and man; redeemer of mankind...) which is and remains unacceptable to almost all Jews. The Jewish religious philosopher Franz Rosenzweig (1886-1929) formulates this: "We are in agreement as to what Christ and his Church signify in the world: no one comes to the Father but through him. No one *comes* to the Father—but it is different when someone does not need to come to the Father because he already *is* with him. And this is the case with the people of Israel (not with individual Jews)."[33]

From the Jewish point of view, the fact that our world is still unredeemed speaks against Jesus's messianism. The medieval rabbis had already pointed this out. For Christians, on the other hand, the redemption, and through it salvation, have already become visible, but are not yet completely realized. That "the whole of creation has been groaning in travail together until now" (Rom 8.22) does not, according to Christian understanding, speak against the redeemer but against the redeemed who only grasp in part or not at all the new way of life manifested by Jesus, and so reject the gift of the redemption.

No dogmatic rapprochement has been achieved between Jews and Christians. But thanks to the discussion of Jewish thinkers about the person of Jesus, Christians have started to reflect on the roots of the faith they profess. Because of their understanding of their faith, Jews cannot see more than a kind of epilogue to the books of the Old Testament in the New Testament writings; but Christians have discovered that the Old Testament is not simply a foreword to the New. In a religious sense both communities have essentially come nearer to each other; the differences in belief are no longer grounds for polemic and denunciation, but can be mutually respected. This only emphasizes the fact that when religious opposites themselves cannot be bridged, the man Jesus himself becomes a bridge which is able to unite both Jew and Christian.

50

3 Son of Man and Son of God: Jesus in Christianity

Some call the man from Nazareth Jesus, others call him Christ. One often comes across the double title of Jesus Christ. For most of us, Jesus and Christ are two proper names for one and the same person. At first this was not so. The name Jesus applied to that man who at the beginning of our reckoning of time lived and was at work in Palestine, and was crucified under the governor Pontius Pilate. In short, Jesus is a proper name. But the term Christ refers to the significance which this Jesus possessed for his followers. Accordingly, "Jesus Christ" is the shortest profession of faith: the man Jesus of Nazareth *is* the Christ. Christós is the Greek translation of the Hebrew word *maschiach* (Messiah) which simply means "the anointed." Very early on this term was considered to be one of the most apposite to describe the being and mission of Christ.

New Testament Profession of Christ

From the start Jesus's followers saw themselves faced with considerable difficulties when it came to defining who Jesus was and what significance would be given to him.[1] The language and conceptual definition at their disposal for this purpose proved to be insufficient. Then an opportunity to speak of Jesus in an adequate way simply presented itself to the authors of the New Testament; they made use of already known concepts, but filled them with a new content. This is well illustrated by the various terms they used to describe Jesus's being and his significance. In theological technical language, these are known as *christological titles*.

(1) For Christians coming from Judaism the most important of these titles was that of *Messiah.* In the Old Testament, messianic hope was not concentrated originally on an individual figure, but on the advent of

God's kingdom. Later, messianic salvation was linked to David's royal family, which is first evident in Nathan's prophecies to King David (2 Sam 7.12-17). The kings, like the priests and to some extent the prophets, were elected to their position by the ceremony of anointing. It is therefore not surprising that a Messiah was seen in every King, for Messiah means "the anointed." After the decline of the monarchy in Israel, the expectation of salvation transferred itself more and more to the future, onto a king who should again bring his people peace and liberty (Is 9.1-6; compare 7.14). Numerous proclamations of the prophets point this way, among them Amos:

In that day I will raise up
David's fallen house
and repair its crumbled walls
and restore its ruins
and rebuild it as in the days of old.
(Am 9.11; Mic 5.1-5; Jer 23.5 ff; Ezek 34.23 ff).

During the Babylonian exile Deutero-Isaiah (the anonymous author of the second part of the Book of Isaiah) announced a "suffering servant of God" as the bringer of salvation, who would take guilt upon himself in place of mankind (Is 42.1-7; 49.1-9; 52.13 ff; 53.12). Zechariah speaks of two messianic figures, of a high priest and a king of peace (Zech 4.11-14; 9.9 ff). And finally in Daniel, God confers sovereignty over the people on "a Son of Man" of divine origin (Dan 7.13 ff).

Although expectation of the Messiah was widespread among the Jews at the time of Jesus, there was no one interpretation of this belief. The zealots who were fighting as partisans against the Roman forces of occupation believed in a political-national leader. Many pious souls hoped for an outstanding teacher of the Law. Others thought that the Messiah would make his appearance as a high priest, a prophet, or an apocalyptic judge.

In the New Testament writings, Jesus is proclaimed as the expected redeemer and savior, that is, as the Messiah. The evangelists particularly make a continuous effort to prove that the prophetic assurances have been realized in him: Jesus was of the house and lineage of David (Mt 1 1; Lk 2.4); he is the Emmanuel proclaimed by Isaiah (Mt 1.23); the suffering servant of God (Mt 12.18-21) of whom Deutero-Isaiah speaks; he is the prince of peace promised by Zecharias (Mt 21.5); the Son of Man, of whom Daniel speaks (Mt 8.20 amongst others). In short, the New Testament is convinced that Jesus is the anointed of God, the Christ, the expected Messiah.

The expected Messiah? Yes — and no. For the evangelists show that Jesus, through his life and his awareness of his mission, has far exceeded all expectations of the Messiah up to now.

(2) In order to emphasize Jesus's messianism, the first Christians employed a whole list of further christological titles which they took from the Old Testament: *servant* (Acts 3.26; Phil 2.7); *prophet* (Lk 7.16; Jn. 6.14; Acts 3.22 ff); *rabbi* (teacher, master: Mt 26.25); *son of David* (Mk 10.47 ff; Mt 21.15); *King of Israel* (Mt 21.5; Lk 19.38); *Emmanuel* (Mt 1.23). This recourse to the Old Testament should not surprise us, as it is known that the first Christian communities came into being within Palestine.

The concept of *Son of Man* had carried more weight over a longer period of time. In Old Testament writings (especially in Ezekiel, but also in Ps 8.5; Job 25.6 and elsewhere) it is used as an exalted expression which describes mankind. In the Book of Daniel a Son of Man comes "with the clouds of heaven" and to him "was given dominion and glory and kingdom" (Dan 7.13 ff). It is possible that the people of Israel are implied by this. It is certain that at the time of Jesus the concept Son of Man did not yet have any clear-cut significance.

There are three groups of "Son of Man" words distinguishable in the synoptic gospels: firstly those which speak of the Son of Man operating in the present (Lk. 9.58: "The Son of Man has nowhere to lay his head"): then those concerned with the suffering Son of Man who will rise from the dead. (Mk 9.31: "The Son of Man will be delivered into the hands of men, and they will kill him; and when he is killed after three days he will rise" — compare Mk 8.31; 10.33; 14.41): and finally prophecies of a Son of Man who will come at the end of time upon the clouds of heaven. This last group of "Son of Man" words is of special significance, in that here the decision of man for or against Jesus is crucial to the decision which the Son of Man, for or against man, will make: "For whoever is ashamed of me and of my words in this adulterous and sinful generation, of him will the Son of Man also be ashamed, when he comes in the glory of his Father with the holy angels" (Mk 8.38; Lk 12.8-10).

53

(3) It is known that apart from the title of Christ (which was very soon taken to be a proper name) none of the Judaeo-Christian titles have gone into the Church's profession of faith. This is because Christianity first started to spread in the Greek speaking Jewish diaspora and in the Hellenistic pagan region. In order to make the significance of Jesus understandable in the Hellenistic cultural area, it became necessary to translate and substitute Palestinian terms and modes of thought. At first the Greek term Kyrios, which means Lord, suggested itself. For the Judaeo-Christians in the diaspora this sovereign name of Lord for Jesus expressed his divinity, because in their Greek translation of the Bible, the Septuagint, the Hebrew name for God, Yahweh, had been rendered by the title of Kyrios.

According to the Old Testament, Yahweh is Lord of the whole world (Josh 3.11; Mic 4.13; Ps 97.5). The form of address "My Lord" is so frequently used as an appeal to God that it is almost the equivalent of a proper name. The New Testament authors describe God as Lord many times, especially when they are quoting the Old Testament. An example of this is Mark's narration of Jesus's entry into Jerusalem: "Hosanna! Blessed is he who comes in the name of the Lord!" (Mk 11.9; Ps 118.25 ff) What is astonishing is that the New Testament authors use the title "Lord" (Kyrios) for Jesus himself and so treat him as an equal to God, the Lord. In that they extol Jesus as Lord, they give expression to their faith in his divinity: "Jesus Christ is Lord" (Phil 2.11).

There are important grounds for believing that Jesus was honored and appealed to as the Lord very early on. Both in the Acts of the Apostles (20.10) and in the first letter to the Corinthians (16.22) we find the ancient Aramaic invocation "Marana tha" which means "Our Lord come!" This prayer call goes back to the liturgical meetings of the original Jerusalem community, from whom Paul presumably took it. For our problem—the significance of Jesus for the first Christians—this Aramaic religious call is important because it proves that Jesus was worshipped as the Lord and so as God, not first by the missionary Gentile-Christians, but in fact by the Judaeo-Christians only a short time after his death.

It is also worth noting that those parts in the Old Testament in which Yahweh is spoken of as the Lord have been applied to Jesus in the New Testament. "Prepare the way of the Lord!" This call which John the Baptist uses for Jesus (Mk 1.3) is a quotation from Isaiah (Is

54

40.3), but by the Lord, Isaiah means Yahweh. When Paul says that everyone that calls upon the name of the Lord will be saved (Rom 10.13) he is thinking of Jesus (Rom 10.9). But the prophet Joel whom Paul is quoting is talking about Yahweh, the God of Israel (Joel 3.5). Numerous other quotations in the New Testament can be cited in which the title of Kyrios is applied to Jesus in order to emphasize his divinity.

(4) Finally one must draw attention to one other New Testament christological title, which was of fundamental significance to the later development of the profession of faith, and even today it is the most widely employed christological formula of faith: Jesus is the Son of God.

At the start of the oldest gospel, Mark, we find this heading: "The beginning of the gospel of Jesus Christ, the Son of God." The question as to whether we are concerned with a copyist's addition does not need to worry us here. The heading is justified, in so far as Mark's gospel is actually structured around the centurion's profession of Christ, which he makes after Jesus's death: "Truly this man was the Son of God!" (Mk 15.39). But what does that mean: Jesus is the Son of God? Two simple references are able to clarify this as not merely a rhetorical question. In Old Testament linguistic usage the people of Israel as a whole are repeatedly described as "God's firstborn Son" or "God's Son" (amongst others, Ex 4.22; Hos 11.1). And according to New Testament understanding, all those who believe in Christ are "sons (children) of God" (amongst others, Gal 3.26; Eph 1.15; Lk 20.36) — which is actually self-explanatory when they pray to God as their common father (Compare Mt 6.9. Lk 11.2)

But when Jesus is mentioned as the Son of God in the New Testament, this concept is used in another sense. This is proved by the fact that the uniqueness of Jesus's being as Son is emphasized in a variety of ways. Paul speaks of Jesus as the "firstborn among many brethren" (Rom 8.29), and of "his Son" (God's) (Rom 8.29), whilst John describes Jesus as the "only Son" (Jn 1.14; 3.16, 18).

(a) Originally Jesus was known as the Son of God in connection with his rising from the dead. Paul's introduction to his epistle to the Romans is a reminder of this. The apostle refers to his calling as "set apart for the gospel of God...concerning his son, who was descended from David according to the flesh and designated Son of God in power according to the spirit of holiness by (literally because of) his resurrection from the dead, Jesus Christ our Lord" (Rom 1.2-4). Jesus is destined to be the Messiah by descent. But he is named Son of God because of his resurrection.

The coronation ritual of the kings of Israel who became "Sons of God" when they ascended the throne served as the introductory model for the naming of Jesus in his sonship. The Second Psalm expresses this clearly. It describes how Yahweh speaks at the enthronement of the king: "You are my son, (as you are now king) today (on the occasion of your enthronement) I have begotten you" (Ps 2.7). We understand from this that enthronement for the king signifies what is resurrection for Jesus: he is named ("begotten") as Son of God. The author of the Acts of the Apostles refers to this introductory model: "And we bring you the good news that what God promised to the fathers, this he has fulfilled to us their children by raising Jesus; as also it is written in the second psalm, 'Thou art my Son, today I have begotten thee.' " (Acts 13.32 ff). Because of his resurrection Jesus is "enthroned" as the Son of God.

(b) Subsequently it was admitted that in the end, this "enthronement" of Jesus is nothing other than a confirmation of his earthly life and work. In other words, one recognizes that Jesus was not first "made" God's Son through the resurrection, but that he had acted with the full authority of the Son throughout his earthly existence. This knowledge is expressed in the accounts of his baptism and his transfiguration. In the synoptic gospels he has already been "adopted" as the Son of God by a "voice from heaven" (and by means of Ps 2.7) at his baptism: "Thou art my beloved Son, with thee I am well pleased" (Mk 1.11). This acceptance of the status of Son is also confirmed at the transfiguration (Mk 9.7).

(c) At what moment of time during his life Jesus could be regarded as the Son of God was a deeply considered question. The next step forward was taken in the Greek communities, where it was remembered that many of the great Old Testament figures had been chosen by God before their birth: Samson, whose birth was announced by an angel to his mother with these words: "for lo, you shall conceive and bear a son" (Judg 13.5); God's servant in Isaiah, who is already called to his service "from the womb" (Is 49.5); Jeremiah, to whom God says:

"Before I formed you in the womb I knew you" (Jer 1.5). Many legends of virgin birth in the contemporary Greek world were harbingers of the divine choice of Jesus from his birth on, especially with regard to the Greek translation of Is 7.14, where one finds: "Behold, a young woman (parthénos) shall conceive and bear a son."[2] The conviction that Jesus is the Son of God found narrative expression in the gospels of his childhood right from the beginning. (Mt 1-2; Lk 1-35).

(d) The consideration that Jesus had always been the Son of God led to further theological investigation and to the doctrine of his pre-existence: even *before* his earthly existence the Son—the "Word," as John says—was with God (Jn 1.1.). This teaching was developed further by an example from an Old Testament pattern of thought. In the book of Job (28.12-27) and in Proverbs (8.22-31) there is an image of Wisdom (who appears almost as a person) existing before God created the world: "When he established the heavens....then I was beside him, as one brought up with him" (Prov 8.27, 30). It was an obvious course to apply this image to Jesus as a testimony of his pre-existence. John was able to consolidate this thought theologically in the famous prologue to his gospel (1.1-18) and in the equally well-known saying of Jesus about the bread from heaven: "for I have come down from heaven" (6.38).

The teaching of the pre-existence, of the incarnation, and of Jesus's elevation is also developed by Paul in his epistles. But long before him they had been a part of the faith, as the hymn to Christ which he quotes in the epistle to the Philippians proves. It was used as a prayer in liturgical assemblies. This hymn starts quietly, it is restrained, almost mysterious. It describes, or rather transcribes, in simple words the earthly work of Jesus and finally flows into a ceremonial profession of him as the Christ and Lord.

Pre-existence: He was in the form of God but did not deem
    equality with God something to be grasped
Incarnation: but emptied himself
    taking the form of a servant
    being born in the likeness of men.
    And being found in human form
    he humbled himself

57

and became obedient unto death
even death on a cross.

Glorification: Therefore God has highly exalted him
and bestowed on him the name
which is above every name,
that at the name of Jesus every knee should bow,
in heaven and on earth and under the earth,
and every tongue confess
that "Jesus Christ is Lord" —
to the glory of God the Father.

(Phil 2.6-11; Col 1.15-20)

From the Christ of the Gospels to the Jesus of History

When Christians today speak of the Son of God who became man, most of them think of the mystery of Christmas: the Son of God came into this world to redeem mankind; we are reminded of the well-known German Christmas carol: "Lord send your son down to us..." But we have already seen that the development of the question 'who is Jesus' does not begin with his pre-existence, nor indeed with his birth, but begins with his resurrection and his elevation to God.

In fact his resurrection was the vital experience for his followers, and it led them to further reflection about his person. To put it more precisely: it was the *meeting* with the resurrected Jesus and the knowledge that he was with God that forced them to enquire again into his being and his significance.[3]

At first Jesus's death could not have been seen as an event of salvation or understood as such. According to the Book of Deuteronomy a "hanged man is accursed by God" (21-23) — a statement that would have been applied to anyone who was hanged on the cross by the Romans at the time of Jesus. In Luke's account of the journey to Emmaus it is evident that Jesus's disciples were stunned and disillusioned, and probably in a state of total despair after his death: "Our chief priests and rulers delivered him up to be condemned to death, and

crucified him. But we had hoped that he was the one to redeem Israel"
(Lk 24.20 ff). To this the risen Jesus (who had not been recognized by
the two disciples) replied: "Was it not necessary that the Christ should
suffer these things and enter into his glory?" Luke continues — "And
beginning with Moses and all the prophets, he interpreted to them in all
the scriptures the things concerning himself " (Lk 20.26). This answer
reflects that process of thought and consolidation which began because
of the appearance of the living Jesus and finally led to the belief in him
as Emmanuel and Redeemer, as the Messiah and Son of Man, as Kyrios
and the Son of God. *This is the faith which lies at the basis of the New
Testament's interpretation of his person.* To put it in plain English,
Jesus never used these christological titles about himself (with the possible exception of Son of Man).

   At this point we must interrupt our train of thought. The profession
of Jesus as the Messiah, the Son of God, Lord and Redeemer lies within
the sphere of faith; these are *dogmatic* statements. Whether and how
Jesus lived is an *historical question* which historians, aided by exegesis,
have to deal with. From numerous sources other than the Bible, it can
be proved that Jesus did in fact live. Several Jewish and other non-
Christian writers of antiquity mention him in their works.[4] Even if they
do not say much about him, these non-Christian witnesses constitute a
proof of his existence independent of Christian sources. In the meantime, the most important sources of research on the life of Jesus are the
New Testament writings, above all the gospels. But it is not possible to
assemble a biography of Jesus from them. They tell us nothing about
the greater part of his life. Apart from one or two episodes from his
childhood, the evangelists begin with the appearance of John the Baptist and Jesus's public activity. As far as the latter is concerned, the differences between the evangelists are in part so considerable that the
events cannot be reconstructed any more, or if so, then only approximately. An example: according to the first three evangelists, Jesus's
public activities lasted about a year to a year and a half; according to the
author of John's gospel, two and a half to three.[5] These divergences
stem from the fact that the evangelists never intended to present only
the bare historical facts. Instead they used the manifold oral and written
traditions, which in their turn, were influenced by the professions of
faith, the liturgy, missionary sermons and the catechesis of the various
Christian communities from which they originate. Besides, the New
Testament authors wrote their works with the intention of proclaiming

the faith in Jesus as the Christ, and to protect this faith from misinterpretation, which naturally influenced their manner of presentation. And finally in this spirit they felt themselves compelled to answer questions which had not been put during Jesus's lifetime. In their eyes it was entirely legitimate for them to put words and directives into Jesus's mouth which did not come from him, but which could have arisen from his way of living and his teaching. To put it more precisely: the gospels were written by men of faith, to strengthen the faithful in their faith and to lead the faithless towards the faith.

Clearly this does not mean that there is nothing to be said about the historical Jesus. Quite the contrary. Bible scholars have developed methods which enable us to venture from the proclamation of Jesus by the critique of editing. This aims at establishing from which standpoint the New Testament authors selected their oral and written transmissions, assembled and adapted them. The critique of tradition researches the various stages of these transmissions and their origin, while the critique of form is interested in and attempts to ascertain in which context the various literary forms of the individual textual units (similes, parables, miracles, debates, hymns...) were originally used. Finally, with the aid of the critique of literature, later alterations, insertions and revisions can be located.

By means of this scholarship it is possible in many cases to ascertain whether individual words and works of Jesus described in the gospels can be traced back either completely or in their nucleus to Jesus himself, or whether they are theological or catechetical statements about Jesus, which the evangelist has incorporated into his work. Painstaking attention to detail has enabled Bible scholars to reach a number of sure conclusions.

It is certain that Jesus was born during the reign of Herod the Great — that is, not after 4 BC. His home town was Nazareth. He was crucified under Pontius Pilate who was the Roman procurator in Judaea from 26-36 AD. The year of his death cannot be established definitely, and even less, the actual day of his death over which John and the synoptic gospels disagree. Both traditions name Friday as the day of execution. According to Mark this Friday was the first day of the feast, that is the 15th day of the Passover month Nisan (Mk 14.12), while according to John it was the 14th day of Nisan, that is the day before the feast (Jn 13.1, 29; 18.28; 19.31).[6]

It is also certain that Jesus was about thirty when he began his public activities, which according to John lasted almost three years, according to the synoptic gospels at least one to two years. Jesus's preaching can be summarized in the concept of the Kingdom of God (Mk 1.4 ff) of which he spoke in numerous parables. What is new in his preaching is that he associated his person with God's Kingdom (Mt 12.28). There is no doubt that Jesus worked miracles—as some of his contemporaries also did (Mt 12.27)—which he interpreted as acts of God and as a sign of God's Kingdom which had begun. The healing of the sick should be mentioned here, and (possibly) of those who were thought to be possessed.

Jesus's keeping company and dining with sinners, or people who were considered sinners because they did not know the rules of the Law and therefore could not observe them, is also verifiable. The defamation which his behavior brought—"Behold a glutton and a drunkard, a friend of tax collectors and sinners" (Mt 11.19; Lk 7.34; Mk 2.16)—has borne the close examination by the historical critique, and shows at the same time that Jesus was "no repentance preacher who wanted to transform all Palestine into a monastery for ascetics."[7]

In principle Jesus rejected neither tradition, nor the Sabbath, nor the purification rules, though he put them in context, for "the Sabbath was made for man, not man for the Sabbath" (Mk 2.27). According to most exegetes, these are the authentic words of Jesus.

It was not because of the conduct of the Jewish people but because of pressure from the Jewish authorities that Pilate sentenced Jesus to death. We are thrown back on hypotheses about the concrete grounds which the authorities used to render Jesus harmless. It is probable that in his preaching and behavior he questioned the ruling religious system of the time, and thus the interests of the ruling religious leaders.

Jesus's resurrection eludes historical research; it is not described by any of the evangelists. On the other hand the assertion that the risen Jesus appeared is historically sure—and the fact that the disciples believed in his rising from the dead.

61

It may now be clearer as to what is involved in a critical reading of the texts of the gospels: namely, the proof that Jesus's claim to be the promised savior was raised by him himself and not simply accredited to him by others after his death. In other words, it is valid to demonstrate that the christological titles—Son of God, Messiah, Lord, Redeemer—which Jesus did not use for himself, are grounded in his actions and in his preaching. Or to put it another way, it must be obvious from Jesus's behavior that to express belief in him as the Son of God represents the legitimate development of the way he saw himself.

Because it has been possible for modern exegesis to trace back the evangelists' image of Christ to the historical Jesus, it is also possible for it to establish the continuity between the claim that the man from Nazareth raised for himself, and the Christ proclaimed by the Church. But of what does this claim, with which Jesus faced his contemporaries, consist? And in what form did he raise it?

(1) At first sight, Jesus does not seem to differ from a rabbi or a prophet or a wise man as they appeared during his time. But he does not talk like them; he commands an authority that no one before him possessed: "You have heard that it was said to the men of old...but *I* say to you..." (Mt 5.21 among others). Other teachers merely commented on the Law, Jesus interprets it as binding. He also does not say, as the prophets of the Old Testament did, "The Word of God" or "A Saying of the Lord" but "Amen Amen, I say to you" (Mt 5.18 among others).

Even if some of Jesus's "Amens" must be taken as a means of educating the community, we should not overlook an astonishing fact. "Amen" serves as a confirmation of a sermon from other preachers, and is therefore spoken at the end. But Jesus—and here we are on historical ground—uses this Amen as an *introduction* to some of his sermons. That means that in contrast to other prophets, he does not speak in the name of God but in his own name, thereby implicitly emphasizing his equality with God.

(2) This second point concerns Jesus's behavior. It is possible that he never *expressly* forgave sins. But it is certain that he was in the habit of dining with tax collectors and sinners—unheard of behavior for the Judaism of that time. Company at table had a religious character. It

signified company, not only with one another, but also before God. This is why Jesus was attacked. Through his behavior he showed sinners that they were not rejected by God. In that he accepted them, he allowed them to *experience* forgiveness. By doing this, he was opposing the prevalent behavior, and also showing that he considered himself to be the authorized representative of God's will. He identified his actions with God's actions. That his contemporaries should have understood this as they did stems from the accusation of blasphemy, which runs like a thread through the various traditions and which also represents the main point of the charge against him in his trial (Mk 2.7; 14.64; Jn 15.18; 10.33).

(3) Furthermore, Jesus's (implicit) claim to be the Messiah shines out in the manner in which he calls the disciples to be his successors. One had to apply to join a Jewish rabbi and was then accepted into his circle of students, in order to become a teacher oneself. This was not the case with Jesus. He chose his apostles freely, and not because they would themselves become masters (rabbis). On the contrary: "But you are not to be called rabbi, for you have one teacher" (Mt 23.8). What counts is solely the radical following of Jesus, the belief in his person. This belief has only one meaning if Jesus really understands himself to be the savior, the redeemer of mankind. In other words, salvation is bound solely to him. That implies a consciousness of messianism within Jesus.

(4) This consciousness of self as the Messiah in Jesus also finds expression in the fact that he attached messianic significance to his death.[8]

(5) The evangelists make a meticulous distinction between Jesus's relationship to God and that of his disciples. When Jesus teaches them the Lord's Prayer he says "But when you pray...pray to your father..." (Mt 6.6). Otherwise he speaks without exception either of "my father" (Mk 14.36; Mt 11.25) or "your father" (Lk 6.36; 12.30, 32; Mk 11.25), a distinction which finds its classic expression in the formulation "my father and your father" (Jn 20.17). Historically seen, this distinction goes back to Jesus himself and gives expression to his exceptional consciousness of the Son.

Sense can only be made of all these speculations on the being of Jesus when they simultaneously make some kind of a statement about his function. To express it differently, the doctrine of Jesus Christ (christology) should not be separated from the doctrine of salvation

63

and the redemption of mankind (soteriology), as, strangely enough, has been done over the centuries in both theological studies and in preaching.

When Christians perceive the savior in Jesus, at one and the same time they express their belief that humanity is already redeemed. Here we are faced with a problem which the Christian teaching of redemption seems to be solving from within itself: how can one believe in a redemption which has already begun when one has the daily experience that our world is still torn and in conflict? The salvation that Christ believed in is indeed more hoped for than present. Jesus certainly preached the Kingdom of God as a reality that has already dawned, but is not yet remotely within reach of perfection. In Jesus Christ, the believer has the promise of the completed redemption. This dynamism between 'already' and 'not yet' runs through the whole of the New Testament (Jn 5.24; 5.28; 6.39 ff). Paul has reappraised it theologically:

"We know that the whole creation has been groaning in travail together until now; and not only the creation, but we ourselves, who have the first fruits of the Spirit, groan inwardly as we wait for adoption, as sons, the redemption of our bodies. For in this hope we were saved. Now hope that is seen is not hope. For who hopes for what he sees? But if we hope for what we do not see, we wait for it with patience." (Rom 8.22-25.)

Paul speaks to his fellow-Christians here about a new experience: the tension which occurs between hoped for salvation and present-day suffering. In no way does Christianity ignore the broken world; but takes it all the more seriously because of its great contrast to enduring perfection. The faithful have not been promised "a brave new world" and an existence without pain. Faith does not disguise the negative aspects of this globe, but to a certain extent it relativizes them, because it offers the certainty that neither pain nor suffering nor death will have the last word: God reserves this word for himself.

Accordingly, Christian teaching on redemption means that the new life should come to pass under the conditions of the old. Whether these conditions can be altered for the better depends on how human beings use them; they are not able to compel the coming of the Kingdom of God through their own strength. But it can be prayed for and assumed (Mk 10.15), and with it, salvation (Mt 6.10). God does not redeem a person against his will and without his cooperation. Jesus himself main-

64

tains this in a short parable: it is pure, unearned coincidence that the man finds the treasure hidden in the field and the merchant finds the exceptionally beautiful pearl. But both of them must sell their possessions to be able to own what they have found (Mt 13.44-46).

Only by practical proof can the Christian convincingly refute the objection that the world is still unredeemed. That implies that for the believer, the teaching of redemption has consequences, not only in regard to his individual expectations of hope, but also with regard to his position within the social system, in public institutions, and in political developments. Questions about economic order, workers' participation, equal rights for both sexes, foreign aid, and environmental conservation are related to justice and compassion, and therefore with the fulfilment of God's will in the prevailing social conditions. In their resolution "Our Hope," the general synod of bishops in Germany set forth the facts clearly: "The Kingdom of God is not indifferent to world trade prices."

True God and True Man

Up to now our interpretation has shown that the New Testament authors did not make Jesus into the Messiah and Son of God. Instead they developed and clarified his claim to be the savior and messenger of God: a claim about which the historical Jesus may have been less specific, but which he still made for himself. To achieve this end, the evangelists employed a language and conceptuality which their contemporaries could understand. On the one hand they were concerned to emphasize Jesus's godhead — for only God can perform that which the human being cannot perform for himself: bring salvation and redemption. On the other hand they never lost sight of his humanity — for if Jesus were not entirely and completely man, what could his work of redemption have to do with us? But how is it possible to think of the divinity and the humanity in Jesus simultaneously? This question introduces an essentially complicated and confusing history that we only have time to summarize in rough.[9]

(1) The first false christological teaching arose from the difficulty of bringing Jesus's humanity and his godhead into line with each other. Either his true and real being as a man was denied and he was granted

65

an apparent body—Ignatius of Antioch who was martyred early in the second century, raised an objection to this: Jesus then would have suffered only apparently and mankind would have been only apparently redeemed.[10] This is known as *Docetism* (from the Greek dokein = to be apparent). Or it was held that God made the man Jesus of Nazareth his Son only at his baptism or at his resurrection—that is, he was adopted to the place of Son—hence the term *Adoptionism*. However neither of these two theories is expounded in the New Testament. We have already seen that the "Adoption formula" in the resurrection, transfiguration and baptism accounts involve only *single* moments in christological reflection, which extends from Christ's pre-existence to his second coming. Adoptionism, like Docetism, has no place in the New Testament. Jesus never makes an appearance as a kind of disguised God. For the evangelists, Jesus is a full and complete man; he experiences needs, such as hunger (Mt 21.18), and thirst (Jn 4.6; 19.28), tiredness and exhaustion (Mk 4.38; Jn 4.6); and shows human emotions—anger and dejection (Mk 3.5), mourning (Mt 26.37) and joy (Lk 10.21), disturbance (Jn 11.33) and pain (Lk 19.41; Jn 11.35). The evangelists emphasize Jesus's humanity in a drastic way in the account of the Passion; Mark and Matthew particularly draw attention to the experience of God forsaking him on the cross (Mk 15.34; Mt 27.46; see also Ps 22.2. and Heb 5.7). The problem lay more accurately in testifying to the godhead in the *man* Jesus. That is why Luke and John, from fear of being misunderstood, replaced Jesus's death cry "My God, my God, why hast thou forsaken me?" (the beginning of Ps 22) with other quotations from the psalms. In Luke Jesus prays: "Father, into thy hands I commit my spirit" (Lk 23.46; Ps 31.6) and in John he dies with the call: "It is finished" (Jn 19.30; Ps 22.23).

(2) The question as to how the divinity and the humanity of Jesus react upon each other finally led to the first great crisis that Christianity had to overcome. It is linked with the name of Arius who was born c.260 in Libya. He received a brilliant education in Syrian Antioch, at that time one of the most important centers of culture in the east. Later he served as a priest in the port of Alexandria on the western bank of the Nile delta. He was widely known as a saintly priest and a great scholar. From about 315 on, in sermons, letters and poems, he held the opinion that unlike the Father, Christ had not existed from all eternity. It was more probable that God had created him from nothing, and then allowed him to take part in the creation of the world. Of course for

Arius, Christ was more than only a man—but at the same time he was less than God, because he was subject to him. The theological term for this is *subordinationism*. According to it the Son would not be godly but at least godlike and therefore the highest and noblest of all *creatures*. Arius's theory was completely in accordance with a philosophical movement prevailing at the time, in which God's thoughts were so much of the world to come that he could not enter into a relationship with the material world, and therefore needed a mediator.

When Arius put his opinions into writing (the "Taáleia," which means a feast) and published them, he was excommunicated by his bishop and fled to Palestine. Later he was reinstated and returned to Alexandria.

In the meantime the controversy had divided people into two camps to such an extent that the Emperor Constantine's attention was drawn to it. At short notice and at his own expense he called a Church Council in 325 in Nicaea in Asia Minor to restore unity. At first greater disorder reigned at this Council. The bishops, amongst whom there were many courageous defenders of the faith but also many obtuse theologians, had the greatest difficulty fending off the numerous and verbose persons—some of them non-believers—who offered their services as speakers. The Council sat in the presence of a papal representative in the palace of the Emperor who presided.

The lengthy debates were actually concerned with the single letter, 'i'. This was not quibbling. The discussions were held in Greek and the question was: is Jesus Christ "homooúsios" or "homoioúsios"—is he the *same* being as God or only *like* this being? Nothing less than the teaching of Jesus's divinity was at stake; the Council fathers finally professed this with a formula which has gone into the Church's confession of faith: Jesus Christ is "God from God, Light from Light, true God from true God...*one being* with the Father" (NR 155). To express it more simply: what is exceptional in the man Jesus is that he belongs entirely and completely on the side of God. Most of the members of the council voted in favor of this confession of faith; the Emperor took care of the rest. Anyone refusing his signature was excommunicated. The writings of Arius and his followers were burnt, and Arius sent once more into exile.

But this did not solve all the problems. The explanatory teaching of Nicaea may have said that divinity and humanity are united in Jesus, but it gave no information about how this unity is to be considered. People began to reflect on the human soul of Jesus — this was new explosive material. Today we understand the soul as a principle of life which moulds and forms the whole human being, and expresses itself through the body. The idea of a body-soul-unity was foreign to the theologians of the time: they thought of a loose association in which the body was seen as a kind of dwelling for the soul, and, moreover, hindered the soul's chance of full development.

Proceeding from these assumptions, a certain Appolinarius from Laodicaea in Asia Minor, tried to explain the link between the divinity and humanity in Jesus. The eternal Logos, the Word that has been with the Father throughout eternity (Jn 1.1) is within Jesus in place of a human soul. According to this, the divine Logos as a principle of life in Jesus would enter into an association with the human body, and together, with Jesus, they would form a single divine nature. The special term for this is *Monophysitism* (from the Greek *mónos* = single; phýsis = nature; that is, the doctrine of one-nature). It seemed unthinkable to Apollinarius that one and the same being should possess two spiritual souls, two principles of the I-consciousness, namely, a divine and a human soul.

In 381, still within his lifetime, Apollinarios's teaching was condemned by the Council of Constantinople. The main argument against the Apollinarists (as his followers were called) was the consideration that Jesus could only be regarded as the Redeemer of all mankind if he himself had become completely and entirely a man, with a human body and a human soul.

Shortly before Apollinarius died, Nestorius was born (c 381 - c 451). He studied theology in Antioch and had such a reputation as a brilliant preacher that even the Emperor Theodosius II took notice of him. In 428 the emperor appointed him Patriarch of Constantinople. There an intense quarrel was in progress, provoked by two pious Marian preachers, who extolled Jesus's mother as "Mother of God." Many people were quite unable to countenance the thought that God could have had a mother: they saw simply a "Mother of man" in Mary. Nestorius tried to mediate and suggested the title "Mother of Christ." But as none of the parties would give way, Nestorius had them all against him. Naturally in the imperial city of Constantinople, the ordinary people took a lively part in this argument. Fighting broke out in the streets, church services were disturbed and organized groups of speakers interrupted the preachers. Nestorius was accused of splitting Christ into two persons, a divine one and a human one, who would then co-exist in a loose association with each other. For if Mary were only Christ's and not God's mother, it would mean that she had only given birth to the man Jesus and not at the same time to God's eternal Word, the Logos. Indeed some of Nestorius's misleading comparisons must have created the impression that, in spite of assurances to the contrary, he was in reality dissolving the inner union between the man Jesus and the divine Logos; the humanity of Jesus, he said, is, so to speak, the garment worn by the divine; it is at the same time the temple in which the divine dwells; it is a tool which the divine uses.

Although Nestorius emphasized the unity between the divinity and the humanity of Jesus he was not able to conceptualize it. One of his contemporaries was to show more skill in this undertaking; Bishop Cyril, who as Patriarch of Alexandria was Nestorius's rival, because Alexandria envied Constantinople the honored position she had claimed for hserself. Since the Council held there in 381, Constantinople had been described as "the second Rome." If Nestorius was considered a gifted preacher, Cyril was an astute theologian. He recognized the theological errors that could come from Nestorius's misleading statements. These created the impression that the Logos had taken on flesh, as if God were to have only a habitat in the man Jesus. Cyril on the other hand, referring to the Prologue in John, emphasized that the Logos became flesh. Divinity and humanity are both present in Christ in equal completeness, and have the closest association with each other.

As this quarrel about the correct teaching was not only between Nestorius and Cyril but threatened to split the whole of the Christian world into two camps, the Emperor Theodosius II called a general church meeting for Whitsun in 431 at Ephesus in Asia Minor, which would re-establish unity. Nestorius's teachings were condemned at this Council, and he was removed from the office of Patriarch of Constantinople. The Council fathers expressly granted Mary the title of "God's Mother," a term which in this connection, however, stated nothing about Mary's position in the divine plan for salvation, but sought to circumscribe the being of Christ. The Church Council also gave its opinion on the being of Christ, in that they ceremoniously approved a letter of Cyril's to Nestorius, in which the former summarized the teaching on Jesus's divinity and humanity:

69

"Although the natures (the divine and human nature of Christ), which were bound together in a true unity, are different, they have truly become *one* Christ and Son. It is not as if the difference between the natures were to have been dissolved for the sake of this union, but that divinity and humanity together have formed the *one* Lord and Christ for us, in consequence of an inexpressible and mysterious fusion into one unity....For it is firstly not an ordinary man who was born of the holy Virgin and upon whom the Word then descended, but he emerged from the womb itself united" (NR 172).

This text expressly emphasizes that in Jesus Christ divinity and humanity are united to each other in an innermost and "inexpressible and mysterious fusion." Of what nature then, is this fusion? How are we to understand the statement that Jesus Christ is entirely and completely God and at the same time completely and utterly man? A conceptual answer was finally decided upon after many lengthy discussions in the year 451 at the Council of Chalcedon, a town on the Bosphorus opposite Constantinople:

"The one and the same Son is perfect according to the divinity and according to the humanity, true God and true Man....The one and the same is consubstantial with the Father according to his divinity, and consubstantial with us, according to his humanity...We profess one and the same Christ, the Son, the Lord, the only begotten, who consists of two natures, unalloyed, unchanged, undivided and inseparable. The difference between the natures will never be relinquished because of their union, it will rather preserve the characteristic quality of each nature (i.e. the divine and the human), in that both come together in one person." (NR 178)

Today this text sounds extremely complicated. This is because the members of the Council in Chalcedon used the philosophical terms understandable at the time. Firstly they reinforce the teaching of Nicaea in that they emphasize Jesus's divinity; the Son is "of one being" with the Father. Then they attempt to explain how Jesus's divinity and his humanity relate to the three-in-one God. They make use of the terms "Nature" and "Person." The term Person refers to *who:* that is, the second divine Person, the eternal Son of God, the Logos. The term Nature on the other hand, refers to *what* the eternal Son of God who became Man unites within himself, namely, divinity and humanity. His divinity is consubstantial with the Father. But as he took our human nature upon himself, he is also consubstantial with us—except of course in sin (Heb 4.15).

70

But the Dogma of Chalcedon only illuminates single aspects of the mystery of Christ. The Council fathers felt themselves obliged to take up a position against certain false interpretations, which either questioned the complete humanity or the true divinity of Christ. In this respect we are simply dealing with a protective formula.

It could be said that the dogmatic development of the Church's teaching about Christ came to an end with the Dogma of Chalcedon. That does not mean, however that theological absorption in this mystery of faith came to an end. For what is valid for the teaching pronouncements of the Church in general also affects the dogma of Christ: what is binding for the faithful is not the wording of a dogmatic decision, but what is meant by it.

Portrayals of Christ

The early Church's dogmas of Christ do not reveal a rounded portrait of him. From the outlines sketched by the New Testament authors the earliest interpreters were able to work out some individual features, stress certain aspects or emphasize other details in stronger colors. This was not to change for centuries. That there is no supertemporal, and in this sense universal portrait of Christ, but only portraits dependent upon a given time can be clearly seen in depictions by painters, who were not entirely uninfluenced by church teaching.[11] These portraits range from the beardless and youthful shepherd of the early Church's catacomb art to the timeless enthroned Imperator and Cosmocrator, to the Christ the King and the Judge of the World of the Romanesque portals and apses. It was not until the 13th century that artists dared to represent Christ crucified with a crown of thorns, and so draw attention to his suffering. In Dürer and Grünewald we are confronted by a cruelly tortured Man of Sorrows; Catholic late Baroque favored sentimental Sacred Heart portraits. In the 18th century Jesus can be seen as an apothecary administering the power of virtue, and from there it is but a short step to the limp portraits of the French and German Nazarene. Important painters of our century have changed direction entirely—among others, Beckmann, Corinth, Nolde, Rouault, Barlach, Matisse, Chagall...

There are theological and religious-pedagogical reasons for this great variety, which are closely linked to each other. As Jesus is more than a mere man, he defies all the usual conceptions of a man. For some it has been possible to proclaim and to actualize him and his teaching in various and constantly changing socio-cultural contexts. Even in the gospels we find different images of Jesus which complement each other. Mark represents Jesus predominantly as a miracle worker; about a third of his material is made up of miracles. In Matthew Jesus appears mostly as a teacher (rabbi). Luke, more than the others, underlines Jesus's predilection for sinners—and thus his compassion. He is the only evangelist to have recorded the parables of the lost silver coin (drachma) (15.8-10), of the Prodigal Son (15.11-32), of the pharisee and the tax collector (18.9-14) and the meeting between Jesus and the chief tax collector Zacchaeus (19.1-10). For John, Jesus is principally the revealer who "has made him (God) known" to man. (1.18)

These various points of emphasis which led to different images of Christ were necessary, because the evangelists had to adapt their message to the understanding of their followers. Jesus's figure and his message were to become matters of contemporary interest: as we have seen, the early church councils were later to attempt such a work of interpretation.

The same can be said of the christological reflection of later centuries, which found expression in the various Christian models of piety, that simply represent the contemporary understanding of the single mystery of Christ, with one distinct image of him in the background. This is the case even when no obvious explanation presents itself. An example would be the spirituality of a Francis of Assisi (1182-1226) whose intention was to interpret the gospel radically during his life, and who therefore was moulded neither by the supertemporal "evangelical Christ figure" nor by the image of the exalted Lord nor the coming Judge of the World, but predominantly by the image of the poor and suffering Jesus.

Present day theological reflection and church teaching is just as incapable of developing an image of the whole Christ as were the early church dogmas or the manifold models of piety which developed during the course of the centuries. No theological work concerned with Jesus can be disinterested, because of the belief that he is the savior, "and there is salvation in no one else" (Acts 4.12). In practice this implies that Christian theology and teaching have to include and clarify man's concrete experiences of evil, in their reflections that (and to what extent) Jesus is the savior in these situations. Seen from this angle it is no longer astonishing that in some new christological versions, Jesus is represented as helper and liberator, or as an exemplary human being or brother. By their nature, such versions cannot contain within them everything that there is to be said about Jesus Christ. They are already limited by their representations. But so long as it is made clear that Jesus is more than a mere helper, more than a liberator or exemplary man or brother, there is no need to speak of reducing or weakening christological dogma. If God is to remain God, he will always be greater than anything the human being can think or say of him.[12] We find this in the doctrine of Jesus's divinity—that every statement about him, whether it be an official teaching or one from an individual theologian—is fragmentary and therefore needs to be supplemented.

Many Christians today have difficulty with the christological titles from the New Testament and, faced with trying to understand the early church dogmas of Christ, they see themselves confronted by almost insuperable difficulties. Terms used in the past, like "Nature," "Person," "Being," "Consubstantial" are now partly invested with other meanings. This implies that today we are in a position to express the early definitions of the church councils in other terms—or for the sake of comprehension we would actually have to express them quite differently. Karl Rahner has observed:

"When someone experiences a metaphysical dizziness at the sentence 'God is Man' and it paralyses his courage to believe, he should simply and bravely say: God has promised me himself entirely and irrevocably in Jesus; this statement cannot be made obsolete or retracted anymore, in spite of the endless possibilities that are actually at God's disposal; he has set a goal for the world and its history and he himself is that goal; and this thought is not only present in the eternal thoughts of God; it has already been established in the world and in history by God himself, in Jesus, the crucified and the risen Jesus. He who says this believes exactly what the christology of the church...wishes to say to him."[13]

Rahner makes a similar statement about the Christian way of life: "When the moral personality of Jesus makes such a real and forceful impression on someone in both word and life that he can find the courage to trust this Jesus unconditionally in life and in death, and so to believe in the God Jesus, then he has gone far beyond a broad humanitarian interest in Jesus and lives (perhaps not introspectively, but truly) an orthodox christology."[14]

73

4 Allah's Prophet and Envoy: Jesus in Islam

The attitude of the Jews towards Jesus underwent an immense change over the centuries, embracing the whole spectrum, from non-observance to a more or less open rejection, to rediscovery and returning him to Judaism. No such change can be observed in the history of Islam. Jesus—Isa—has received attention from the followers of Muhammad only in so far as he is mentioned in the Koran.

"Jesus, whom they (the Muslims) do not recognize as God, they revere however as a prophet, and they revere his Virgin Mother Mary; from time to time they call out to her piously." This comment from the Council's Declaration "The Relationship of the Church to Non-Christian Religions" (No. 3) is not concerned to make a summary of what the Koran teaches about Jesus, but simply to point out that Jesus is regarded as a prophet in Islam. Only by a careful analysis of the relevant parts of the Koran can his role as prophet be precisely determined.

Episodes About Jesus

These texts are not in chronological sequence and cannot be fitted together to make a life history of Jesus. They are more concerned with single episodes about his activities, which suggest a particular image of him. In order to trace this, we will not proceed chronologically in the sense of considering at what time the individaul Suras originated, nor will we follow the order into which these Suras have been put in the final edition of the Koran. Instead we will make use of the biography given us by the evangelists, from the birth of Jesus to his death.

An early Koran text in which the birth of Jesus's mother is described lies outside our scope (Sura 3.33-37). Mary is the daughter of Imran and Hanna, who dedicates her unborn child to Allah. The father dies before the birth of the daughter. As a child Mary is taken to a corner of the temple, and there she is brought up by her uncle Zacharias. Whenever he goes into Mary's corner, he finds that his niece has been miraculously

74

provided with food. Such stories have a special literary function. Through the depicting of unusual episodes in the mother's life, the reader or listener is prepared for the son's exceptional mission. Seen from the viewpoint of religious history, the story of Mary's childhood makes use of a common device: the splendor that a great personality radiates is also transferred to his surroundings, to relations or to parents. The account of the birth and childhood of Mary, also well known among the Christian store of legends, is not commented on by the evangelists, but there are parallels in the New Testament apocrypha.[2]

Parallels to the apocrypha and to the gospels are also found in one of the two Suras which relate the annunciation of Jesus's birth. The following summary documents what is obvious.

Sura 3.42-51	Luke's Gospel. Ch. 1	The Protoevangelium of James Ch. 11
42 The angels said: "O Mary! verily God has chosen thee and has chosen thee above the women of the world.	28 And he (the angel Gabriel) came to her and said: 'Hail, O favored one, the Lord is with you.' 42 And she (Elizabeth) exclaimed with a loud cry: 'Blessed are you among women...'	1 A voice said: 'Hail, most blessed among women. 2 You have found grace before the Almighty.'
43 O Mary be devout unto thy Lord and adore with those who adore."	38 And Mary said, 'Behold, I am the handmaid of the Lord.'	3d And Mary said: 'See, I am the maid of the Lord before him.'
44 This is one of the secrets of the unseen world which we reveal to you though you were not there when they cast lots to determine which of them should take care of Mary nor were you with them when they argued about this.		'to throw lots.' (Compare Protoev. 9.9: The priest of the temple said to Joseph: 'Joseph, you have been assigned through your lot the virgin of the Lord: take her under your protection.')
45 The angel said,"O Mary, truly God gives you the glad tidings of a word from him.	(Compare Jn 1.14; 'And the Word was made flesh.')	

75

Sura 3.42-51	Luke's Gospel. Ch. 1	The Protoevangelium of James Ch. 11
His name shall be the Messiah, Jesus the son of Mary, and regarded in this world and the next with those whose place is near to God.	31-32 ...and you shall call his name Jesus. He will be great...	3b What shall be born of you will be holy, and named Son of the most High. And you shall call him Jesus.
46 He shall preach to people in his cradle and when he has grown up he shall be among the righteous.''		(Arabian Childhood Gospel 1.1: Jesus spoke (already) as he still lay in the crib)
47 She said, "Lord, how can I have a son when man has not yet touched me?" He said, "God creates what he pleases. When he decrees a thing he need only say 'Be,' and it is.	34 And Mary said to the angel, 'How shall this be, since I have no husband?' 35 And the angel said to her, 'The Holy Spirit will come upon you, and the power of the Most High will over-shadow you.'	2 I shall conceive the Lord, the living God (and bear) as every woman bears? 3a And the angel of the Lord said: 'Not so, Mary, for the power of the Lord will over-shadow you.'
48 And he will teach him the Book, and wisdom, and the law and the gospel and he shall be a prophet to the people of Israel, saying		
49 'I have come to you with a sign from God: I will create out of clay the form of a bird and I will blow thereon and it shall become by God's per-mission a living bird	33 And he will reign over the house of Jacob for ever: (compare Mt 1.21: 'for he will save his people from their sins.')	3c He will save his people from their sins. (James's gospel does not relate the story of the bird, but it is found in the accounts of childhood in Thomas
I will heal the blind and lepers and raise the dead to life and I will tell you what you eat and what to store up in your houses. That will be a sign for you if you are believers.	In answer to John the Bap-tist's question as to who he is, Jesus (Lk 7.22) replies: 'Go and tell what you have seen and heard: the blind receive their sight, the lame walk, lepers are cleansed, and the deaf hear, the dead are raised up, the poor have good news preached to them.	(2.2-4): The five-year-old Jesus forms sparrows out of clay, then claps his hands to bring them to life. The Ara-bian Childhood Gospel tells the same story, ch. 36)

76

Sura 3.42-51	Luke's Gospel. Ch. 1	The Protoevangelium of James Ch. 11
50 I will confirm the Torah already revealed and will make lawful for you some of that which was prohibited. I have come to you with a sign from your Lord so fear God and follow me for God is my Lord and your Lord, so worship him. This is the right path.' "	(Compare Lk 16.17: 'But it is easier for heaven and earth to pass away than for one dot of the law to become void.')	

Another part of the Koran describes the annunciation of Jesus's birth:

And make mention in the Book, of Mary when she went eastward, apart from her people and took a veil to shroud herself and We (Allah) sent Our spirit (the angel Gabriel) to her who assumed the form of a full-grown man. She said: "I fly for refuge from you to the God of Mercy and if you fear Him leave me."

He said: "I am only a messenger from the Lord, that I may bestow on you a holy son."

"How shall I bear a son," she said, "when no man has touched me?"

"This is the Lord's will. Nothing is difficult for Him. The Lord has said: 'He shall be a sign for mankind and a blessing from us. We have so decreed.' " (19.16-21)

The name of the "full-grown man" who announces the birth of a son to Mary is not given, but early on, Islamic tradition had identified him as the Archangel Gabriel.

In Luke (1.26-38) there is a clear distinction between the promise of the birth of Jesus and the conception which is spiritually engendered, but in the Koran it seems that these two events are made one. The question as to how Islam understands the conception of Jesus cannot be answered with any clarity. According to the Koran, it can only be firmly established that Jesus is called into being through the almighty creative word of Allah. "God forbid that He Himself should beget a son! When he decrees a thing He need only say: 'Be,' and it is" (19.35). According to the Koran, the begetting of Jesus is to be compared with the creation of Adam, who also had no bodily father: "Jesus is like Adam in the sight of Allah. He created him of dust and then said to him: 'Be,' and he was" (3.59). Some interpreters of the Koran hold the view that the Archangel Gabriel begot Jesus in a most unusual way. Mary conceived as she put on her tunic which Gabriel had breathed on.[3] But this is an interpretation that has no basis in the text itself. Jesus's birth is also described in the Koran:

> So she conceived him and she returned with him into a remote place. And the labor pains came upon her at the trunk of a palm tree and she said: "O that I had died before this and been entirely forgotten!" But a voice (according to some interpreters the angel Gabriel, to others the child himself) called to her from below: "Grieve not, for the Lord has placed a stream beneath your feet and if you shake the trunk of the palm tree it will drop ripe dates to gather. So eat and drink and rejoice and if you should see any man say to him: 'I have vowed a fast to the Merciful One and will not speak today with a human being.' " (19.22-26)

This is reminiscent of an episode in chapter 20 of the apocryphal pseudo-gospel of Matthew. During the flight into Egypt, Mary sits down under a palm-tree and desires to eat of the tree's fruit. At the command of the child Jesus the palm bends down until Mary has picked the fruit. At the same time a spring begins to bubble at the foot of the palm. It can be proved that the pseudo-gospel of Matthew was not known in the Orient at the time of Muhammad. On the other hand, the store of legends within the book were in circulation throughout Arabia as it was then.

In contrast to the conception of Jesus, which according to the Koran occurred without the assistance of a man, the birth follows in the most natural way, with pain and birth-pangs (19.23). The doubts that her people voice about Mary and the origin of the child are banished by a miracle. Jesus himself, although still "in the cradle" (19.29) justifies his mother and at the same time clarifies his mission:

> Whereupon he said: "I am a servant of Allah. He has given me the Book and has made me a prophet and has blessed me wherever I go. He has required prayer and almsgiving of me so long as I live. He has told me to honor

78

my mother and has cleansed me of wickedness and vanity. He brought peace upon me the day I was born and he shall do the same the day I die and the day I shall be raised up alive." (19. 30-33)

The power to perform miracles is given not only to the child Jesus in the Koran (he speaks in his cradle 3.46; 19.29; he brings clay birds to life 3.49), but also to the adult preacher. The healing of lepers and the blind as well as the raising of the dead have already been mentioned in the account of the Annunciation (3.49). These miracles are called to mind once more in the 5th Sura, where Allah expressly refers to them as having been performed according to his will:

> O Jesus, son of Mary, remember my favors towards you and towards your mother, when I strengthened you with the Holy Ghost till you did speak to men in the cradle and when grown up. And when I taught you the Book and wisdom and the Torah and the gospel; when you created of clay the likeness of a bird by my power and blew upon it and it became a bird; and you healed those blind from birth and lepers, and with my permission raised the dead to life; and when I protected you from the children of Israel when you came to them with plain signs and the unbelievers among them said: "This is nothing but magic." (5. 110)

Finally, one of Jesus's miracles is called to mind, which serves to identify him as Allah's prophet:

> And when I inspired the disciples that they should believe in Me and in My apostle they said: "We believe, bear witness that we are submissive." And when the disciples said: "O Jesus, son of Mary, is your Lord able to send down a table of food from heaven?" he replied: "Fear God if you are true believers." They said: "We wish to eat of this that our hearts may be at rest and that we may know that what you have told us is the truth and we may be among the witnesses." Jesus, son of Mary, said: "Lord, send down to us a table from heaven for our feast and for those who follow us as a sign from You. Give us provisions for You are the best of providers." Allah replied: "I am sending it down to you but whoever disbelieves among you after that shall be punished as I have not punished any one in all the world." (5. 111-115)

This extract from the Koran still puzzles interpreters today. Presumably Muhammad has honed in on a New Testament tradition which became distorted over the years. What does this account refer to? Some people are reminded of the feeding of the five thousand (the miraculous multiplication of the loaves, as described in Mk 6.34-44), others of the vision of St Peter who saw a great dish with all kinds of animals in it coming down from heaven, and was commanded at once to eat from it (Acts 10.9-16). But it is more probable that it is a distant reminiscence of the Last Supper and (or) Jesus's sermon on the bread from heaven (Jn 6.22-59). In contrast to the other three evangelists, John contains no account of the founding of the Eucharist, but substitutes Jesus's sermon on the bread of heaven, which also refers to the Eucharist. The bread of which Jesus speaks and which he himself is (Jn 6. 35,48) comes "from heaven" (6.32); it is "the bread of life" (6.35); the "Father" (6.37) gives it to mankind who then will not be "cast out" (6.37). At the same time it concerns a test, for many of Jesus's disciples take "offence" at his words (6.61).

Parallels to the text quoted from the Koran come to mind: the "table" concerned comes "from heaven." This event signifies a "feast" which is prepared for all by the "provider" (Allah). At the same time a test is involved: "But whoever of you disbelieves after that shall be punished...."

The Death and Elevation of Jesus

Lastly the Koran mentions Jesus's crucifixion and elevation: "They (the Jews) denied the truth and said a mighty calumny about Mary [some had accused her of sexual offence; see 19.27; 'Mary, this is a strange thing!'] They said: 'Truly we have killed the Messiah, Jesus the son of Mary, the apostle of God,' but they did not kill him for they had only a likeness of him. And they who disagreed about him were in doubt concerning him and knew nothing about him and they did not really kill him but Allah is mighty and wise and took him up to Himself" (4. 156-158).

While the Jews maintain that they have killed Jesus (4.157) the Koran says: "They did not kill him but only a likeness of him" (4.157). This extract has caused interpreters a great deal of trouble over the centuries.

(1) According to popular Islamic belief, another man was crucified in place of Jesus, which implies, from one point of view, that there was a "Doppelgänger," or — from another — a mistake. Tradition has produced various names to support the latter hypotheses: a certain Sergius, Simon of Cyrene, the apostle Judas...

This tradition was evidently known to Muhammad, and in all probability it can be traced back to Christian sects of the 2nd century, who were scandalized that the Son of God should have suffered an ignominious death on the cross. At any rate Irenaeus of Lyon (middle of the 2nd century) contested the view that Simon of Cyrene was crucified in Jesus's place "out of ignorance or because of a mistake."[4]

(2) Other followers of Islam are of the opinion that Jesus himself was crucified. If the Koran denies his death: "they did *not* kill him" (4.157), it is not a contradiction, but is in accordance with the Koran's teaching about other martyrs; namely that they are not really dead: "Never think that those who were slain in the cause of Allah are dead. They are alive, and well provided for by their Lord; pleased with his gifts..." (3.169) With reference to Jesus this means that although his body has been killed, his spirit and his message have not. However the majority of Muslims, the Sunnites, reject this interpretation.

Recently Claus Schedl has come to a similar conclusion in his large-scale study "Muhammad and Jesus": according to the Koran neither Jesus's Doppelgänger nor any other man was killed in his place. The mistake the Jews made lies far more in their failure to "recognize the coming Messiah in Jesus. Although they could crucify the body of the Messiah (in the man Jesus), the nails could not reach the spirit-Messiah, as Allah had exalted him to himself " (compare Sura 3.55).[5]

In fact it is not of real importance to Islamic theology, whether another man died in Jesus's place, or whether a semblance of a body was crucified, or Jesus himself. In contrast to the Christian teaching of redemption, the suffering and death of a god-man in Islam are dispensable elements.

The various interpretations of the crucifixion lead to different explanations about the time of Jesus's death and exaltation. Two texts from the Koran are of prime significance on this point; both are concerned with his exaltation and resurrection.

"....they did not kill him but Allah is mighty and wise and took him up to Himself. There is none among the People of the Book (Jews and Christians) but will believe in him before his death; and on the Day of

Resurrection he will bear witness against them" (the unbelievers of the past) (4.158-159).

"He (Allah) said: 'Jesus, I am about to cause you to die and lift you up to Me. I shall take you away from the unbelievers (from their rebukes) and exalt your followers above them all till the Day of Resurrection. Then to me you shall all return and I shall judge your disputes' " (3.55).

(1) If one accepts that Jesus himself suffered death on the cross (contrary to the opinion of most Muslims), then the elevation to Allah only concerns the "Spirit of the Messiah" (Schedl), who at the end of time will then rise again with the other dead.

(2) If however, one interprets the statement "They did not kill him" (4.157) to mean that another was crucified instead of Jesus, it follows that he was elevated (lifted up) to Allah alive (4.158). His death will then take place at the end of time when he will come again, and all Jews and Christians ("the People of the Book"; 4.159) will believe in him. Jesus then will rise again to a new life at the Last Judgement with the rest of human kind. When the Koran mentions Jesus's resurrection, we know that it is referring to the general rising from the dead on the last day, and not to the events of Easter: "Blessed was he on the day he was born and the day of his death; and may peace be on him when he is raised to life" (19.15; compare 19.33; 3.55).

In the Koran it is said that Christians and Jews alive at the time of Jesus's second coming will believe in him (4.159). Islamic tradition on the other hand has some very concrete details about Jesus's activities during the time between his second coming and his death.[6] Jesus appears in order to announce the Last Judgement. He marries and has children and rules for forty years in Jerusalem. He abolishes everything that runs counter to Islamic belief: he drives away pigs, he destroys churches and synagogues and does away with crucifixes. Peace reigns among men, and also between men and animals. After his death Jesus is buried in Medina beside the prophet.

Jesus the Prophet

What is the significance of Jesus in Islam? This question can best be answered by a comparison between the Christian and Islamic images of Jesus.

82

(1) In view of the manner in which the Koran depicts Jesus's death, we can say that Jesus is not the redeemer of mankind. Islam does not recognize any inherited original sin, upon which the Christian teaching of the necessity of redemption rests. Also the sheer idea of achieving redemption through the sufferings of another is totally foreign to it. Here Christianity and Islam differ radically. According to the Koran (6.164) no one should carry another's burden (sins).

(2) Islam also denies the divinity of Jesus. On the one hand this is linked to its strict monotheism; on the other to a false interpretation of the Christian teaching of the Trinity which, according to an Islamic point of view, implies a belief in three Gods. The polemic of the Koran is therefore not against Christ, but against the Christians who honor him as God:

> "People of the Book (Christians), do not overstep the bounds of your religion. Say nothing against Allah but the truth. The Messiah, Jesus the son of Mary, is but the apostle of Allah and His Word which He cast into Mary; a spirit from Him. Believe then in Allah and His apostles and say not 'Three.' Have done! It were better for you. Allah is only one God. Allah forbid that He should have a son! He is what is in the heavens and in the earth" (4.171).

"Unbelievers are those that say: 'Allah is the Messiah, the son of Mary.' (That implies, only an unbeliever could maintain that Christ is God). For the Messiah himself said: 'Children of Israel, serve Allah, my Lord and your Lord.' He that worships other gods besides Allah shall be forbidden Paradise, and Hell shall be his home. None shall help the evil-doers" (5.72).

Allah is "self-sufficient" (10.68); he needs no female companion and no son: he "has taken no wife, nor has he begotten any children" (7.23.; 6.101). Just how noteworthy Allah's solitariness and omnipotence are is shown clearly in the way he repeatedly acts towards Christ and his mother, who are both only extraordinary people with ordinary human needs: "The Messiah, the son of Mary, was no more than an apostle: other apostles passed away before him. His mother was a saintly woman (no goddess). They both ate earthly food" (i.e. had needs as other people) (5.75).

The Koran then denies not only the divinity of Jesus, but also the god-like qualities of Mary. The following extract expresses this unequivocably:

83

Then Allah will say: "Jesus, son of Mary, have you said unto mankind: 'Take me and my mother as two gods beside Allah'?" Jesus will say: "Glory to You. It is not for me to say that which I know not to be the truth for if I had said that You would have known it. You know what is in me but I know not what is in You. You alone know all things that are hidden" (5.116).

The conclusion seems to be that, according to the Koran, the Christian Trinity includes three deities, namely Allah (Father) Mary (Mother) and Christ (Son). The question as to how Muhammad reached this misunderstanding of the Christian teaching of the Trinity cannot be answered with certainty. Possibly it was contact with certain erroneous forms of Christian piety and/or with the Marian cults of Christian sects in Arabia or Abyssinia.

It emerges from our analysis of the text that the Koran only indirectly discards Jesus as God's son, and thereby indirectly discards his divinity. Statements on this subject are actually directed at proclaiming Allah as the one true God.

If, however, the Islamic misunderstanding of the Christian teaching of the Trinity could once be recognized as such, would it not be possible for Muslims to acknowledge Jesus as the Son of God? This is a legitimate question, but it cannot receive a positive answer. A follower of Islam cannot possibly understand that for Christians the Doctrine of the Trinity does not represent the relinquishing of a belief in one God, but the deepening of it. He cannot follow this because for him the Koran does not represent a text-book which can only be understood correctly when one takes the human assumptions of thought and the historical conditions under which it came about into account. For the Muslim the Koran is far more the immutable Word of Allah, which he passed on to Muhammad through the angel Gabriel—and therefore it is an absolute authority that should not be questioned. While the Christian may ask on which misunderstandings does the Koran base its denial of Jesus's divinity, the mere fact that the Koran rejects as idolatry the honoring of Jesus as God's Son is enough for the Muslim.

(3) In Islam Jesus is not the son of Allah, but the son of Mary. This description of Jesus is frequently used—33 times to be exact—while in the gospel it is found only once (Mk 6.3.). It emphasizes the role of Mary in Jesus's life, and also calls his miraculous origin to mind. Further, Jesus appears as blessed by Allah (19.31); as favored by God

(because he is elevated) (3.45); as noble in this world and in the hereafter (3.45), whereby his power as intercessor is emphasized; he is strengthened with the holy spirit (5.110), which is simply what the Koran also says about "ordinary" believers (see 58.22).

(4) The Koran uses many other descriptions of Jesus, which inevitably call up associations with the gospels for the Christian reader. Jesus is named a Word coming from him (3.45); and Allah's Word (4.171). The significance of these statements does not correspond in any way to the identical formulation in John's Prologue (Jn 1.14) which Christian tradition understands in the sense of Christ's pre-existence with the Father through all eternity. According to Islamic tradition, the extracts we have mentioned from the Koran state that Jesus is the prophet proclaimed through God's word; that he is the concrete fulfillment of that word of the creator that Allah voiced at the annunciation of his birth; that he has preached Allah's word—and nothing more—and lastly, that through his own works he himself represents a "word," that is, a sign from Allah.[8]

Muhammad is not remotely thinking of the content of Christian meaning when he says that Allah calls Jesus "a mortal whom We favored" (43.59). There is absolutely no connection between the Old Testament servant of God (Is 42.1-7; 49.1-9; 50.4-9; 52.13-53, 12), who in the New Testament is identified with Christ the Redeemer (see among others, Phil 2.6-11) and the Christ of the Koran, who is there called God's servant. The contrary is true: Jesus is "no more than a mortal whom We (Allah) favored" (43.59).

The Koran repeatedly terms Jesus the Messiah (almasih). There are also no Christian undertones to be heard in this concept. The Koran expressly blocks the way to any speculation about the New Testament's understanding of the Messiah: "...the Christians say the Messiah is the son of God...God confound them! How perverse they are!" (9.30). In the Koran, Messiah (Christ) had the meaning of a proper name.

(5) Jesus is a prophet (19.30), and thereby is on a level with Noah, Abraham and Moses (33.7). "In the context of other stories of prophets it is shown that all the special features which the Koran ascribes to Jesus have their counterparts or parallels in the prophets before him. So Adam comes into being through a similar act of creation (3.59). Moses awakens the lifeless to life...."[9]

But as a prophet Jesus is also an apostle of Allah (4.157, 171)—and "only an apostle" (5.75). As such he can call upon previous revelation, and is thereby linked to the teaching of earlier prophets: "...We (Allah) sent forth Jesus, the son of Mary, confirming the Torah already revealed, and gave him the gospel in which there is guidance and light, corroborating what was revealed before it in the Torah, a guide and an admonition to the righteous" (5.46; 5.110).

With reference to the Torah, the gospel proclaimed by Jesus brings certain relief (3.50; 4.160) and the clarifying of contentious questions (43.63). Although Jesus, who is "strengthened with the Holy Spirit" (5.110), threatens the fractious with punishment (43.65) only a few listen to him. Among these are his disciples, who turn to their teacher with these words: "We are the helpers of Allah. We believe in Allah. Bear witness that we have surrendered ourselves to Him" (3.52). In the Arabic text the word for believer is *muslimûn* which literally means: that we "are submitted" to God, or that we are Muslims. The same word-play can be found in 3.64 and 5.111.

Jesus was only a proclaimer of Allah's teaching. Muhammad was the first to receive the final revelation and to adhere strictly to it in the Koran. "And Jesus the son of Mary who said to the Israelites: 'I am sent forth to you from God to confirm the Torah already revealed, and to give news of an apostle that will come after me whose name is Ahmad' " (6.61). The name Ahmad has the same meaning as Muhammad; the Praised One.

Naturally in view of the Islamic interpretation of the figure of Jesus, it was impossible for the Christians not to draw attention to the significance of the dogmas of the Incarnation, the Redemption and the Trinity. Both camps published attacks which were in part embittered, and always concerned with the same questions which are still relevant today: falsification of the Bible, respective distortion of the gospels in the Koran: refutation and defense of Christian dogmas; the merits of one's own and respective demerits of the opposing religious practice. Apologetic is all too often reduced to cheap polemic.[10]

A fictitious exchange of letters between two friends is able to illustrate the level to which the confrontation has sometimes descended. Both are in the service of the Caliph, one of them converts to the Christian religion, while the other is a follower of Islamic belief. The author of this document, al-Hasimi, lived early in the ninth century.[11]

The Islamic letter writer praises the faith of Jesus and his disciples, who are proclaimers of the true meaning. Afterwards he threatens his hostile correspondent with hell fire if he doesn't finally desist in his aberrations, renounce his abominations, and turn away from his unbelief. The Christian answer is an echo of these insults: Muhammad was a common robber and murderer. His sexual potency was said to be that of forty men. He was a lecher and a debaucher which explains why he had fifteen wives, and — "how then could the prophet find any time at all to pray?"

This mutual denunciation was followed by condemnation, which led, among other things, to Muhammad being identified in the Christian commentary to the Apocalypse with the anti-christ.[12]

The "Christ of Islam" is the Koran

Dialogue between Christians and Muslims has only been possible since the beginning of this century. Rapprochement has at least taken place on social and cultural levels. Jesus's proximity to God, his ideal of poverty and his life of prayer have indeed been themes of Islamic mysticism over the centuries. Currently one can also discover anew in Islam, the man Jesus, whose spiritual and moral greatness can point the way for all human kind.[13]

A better relationship between Islam and Christianity can only come into being on the basis of mutual respect and tolerance. As for the differences in belief, these are so great that they can only be bridged by one of the two religions paying the price of a loss of identity.

(1) The image of Jesus in the Koran differs essentially from the image of Jesus in the gospels. Muhammad did not get to know and learn to value Jesus by way of Christianity, but through evangelist traditions, apocryphal records (childhood gospels!) and Christian sects which had spread throughout Arabia.

(2) Islam knows many of the Christian terms and honorary titles for Jesus (Son of Mary, Blessed of God, Word made Flesh, Servant of God, Messiah-Christ, prophet, envoy of God) without having absorbed any of the Christian content implicit in them.

(3) The Muslims reject the Christian doctrine of redemption, of sonship of God, of the pre-existence of the Son of God, and of the Trinity.

(4) The Koran gives a stereotypical image of Jesus. But Christians should not overlook "that the gospels have typified a man in a similar way, namely John the Baptist, whom they for their part saw as a

forerunner of Jesus. They too have not left much of the historical reality and, what is worse, of the Baptist's understanding of himself as the envoy of God—who, according to the Muslim view, was just as much of a prophet as Jesus."[14]

(5) As Allah's envoy, Jesus has a high position in Islam; he is the proclaimer of God's will and at the same time he is a forerunner of Muhammad. For he—and not the Jesus of the Christians—is "the envoy of Allah" and so "the Seal of the Prophets" (33.40). But the Koran, which represents a copy of the original heavenly book (56.78; 85.21-22) and is therefore an authority that may not be questioned, is at the same time the "Christ of Islam."[15]

Who Is God?

"Of all the words in our vocabulary, the word God is the most loaded. No other is so sullied, so mauled about."[1] There is something to be said for Martin Buber's observation. Certainly no other word is as hackneyed and at the same time as emotionally loaded as the word God.

God: he has become an object of speculation, an object to be dissected. At times theologians were able to explain his plans so exactly that it was almost as if they had played cards with him every evening. He was plucked out of his mystery and degraded to second-hand goods, sold as a brand, made to serve as an advertisement. God, or rather the word God, was used—and misused—for many things. It is an overburdened word and, for many people, linked to a number of misunderstandings. The experiences connected with it and the images and concepts brought into play by it refer not only to the light side of human existence, but often to the dark as well. That is one of the reasons why it is often difficult to speak of God. Karl Rahner draws our attention to a further difficulty:

"The German word at least, states nothing or nothing more about God. Whether that was always so, in the oldest history of the word, is another matter. At any rate today the word 'God' has the effect of a proper name. One has to know from somewhere else what or who is meant. Often this doesn't occur to us; but it is so. If we would call God, for example, 'Father,' 'Lord' or 'the Heavenly One' or something similar, as clearly happens in the history of religion, then the word 'God' itself would say something about its meaning from its origin in our former experience and from its profane use. For the present though, it looks as if the word is gazing at us like a sightless countenance."[2]

What or who is meant by God only becomes more or less clear from the history of religion, insofar as the individual religions tell of God's actions and thus state something about his being. But even within the three great monotheistic religions, with all their similarities, very different concepts of God are revealed.

"If I had to reduce the faith of Judaism in telegraphic language to three words, I would choose *thirst for unity:* a quenchless thirst for that primal unity which lies at the basis of the sheer inexhaustible diversity of creation. The God of Judaism is one and unique, he who created the universe. The concept of *universum* which means combined in one, whole, although Latin, is based on Hebrew thought. And into this would God put mankind as a great family which stemmed from Adam and is and remains a brotherhood under the one Father-God."[3]

God's oneness is already emphasized in the oldest Jewish profession of faith, the "Schema Jisrael": "Hear, O Israel: The LORD our God is one LORD: and you shall love the LORD your God with all your heart, and with all your soul, and with all your might" (Deut 6.4 ff).

Originally this profession of faith was based solely on the conviction that Yahweh was the one and only God *for Israel*—it certainly did not exclude the existence of other gods. This observation may seem rather shocking to both Christians and Jews, as both believe that there is only one God: but then this belief at the same time fashions the glass through which they read and interpret the Old Testament. They forget that the people of Israel had covered a great distance before they finally found the way towards their profession of faith in the one and only God.

In a most informative study the exegete Norbert Lohfink tells us that the assumption that there were many gods and goddesses was taken completely for granted in the earliest writings of the Old Testament.[4] Also the people of Israel knew that their ancestors had worshipped various gods. The Patriarch Jacob reports that he "said to his household and to all who were with him, 'put away the foreign gods' " (Gen 35.2), and from Joshua we hear that he demands of his countrymen that they "put away the gods which their fathers served beyond the River and in Egypt" (Josh 24.14).

Experts today assume that the Yahweh-God of patriarchical history was a tribal god. Unlike other gods he was not tied to one particular place but could be worshipped everywhere, and also reveal himself everywhere. We are therefore not concerned with a local god but with the god of a people, who accompanied his worshippers wherever they went. When the ancestors, whom we must imagine as nomads and half-nomads, emigrated to the arable land of Palestine (Cana) from the desert and mountainous region between the Red Sea and the Dead Sea and settled there, they were confronted with the concept of a whole heavenly thearchy, at whose head El, the chief god and king of the gods, stood. They transferred this name subsequently to their own god, who was then described as "the God (El) of Abraham, the God of Isaac and the God of Jacob" (Ex 3.6, 15). According to today's calculations, the encounter with the El-God and his gradual equation with the Yahweh-God took place before the exodus from Egypt.

At a time that can no longer be accurately determined, groups of Yahweh worshippers pushed into Egypt and were there obliged to serve the state. Probably at the turn of the 13th century to the 12th century BC, descendants of these immigrants left Egypt under the leadership of Moses, and were able to establish a new existence in the area of the Sinai peninsula. About 1100 BC their descendants pushed through into Palestine and gradually took possession of the land.

We need not concern ourselves here in detail as to how the exodus from Egypt and the acquisition of land in Palestine happened. What is important is that the exodus-experience represented a key experience for the emigrants. They did not understand their flight and the acquisition of land as self-liberation, but as liberation through their God, who revealed himself therefore in a unique way as their deliverer. The memory of this great feat was to find expression in the so-called historical credo:

"...My father was a wandering Aramean who went down to Egypt and, with a small household, lived there as an alien, but they grew to be a great nation. But the Egyptians treated us cruelly and enslaved us and when we cried to the LORD God of our fathers the LORD heard our voice, and looked on our affliction and our oppression. And the LORD brought us forth out of Egypt with a mighty hand and outstretched arm and with great terribleness and with signs and with wonders..And he has brought us into this place and given us this land, a land flowing with milk and honey" (Deut 26. 5-9).

The knowledge that Israel's God is not tied to a place but is like a person and supportive of persons and can therefore be called upon and experienced everywhere and in every situation as a helper and protector has also found expression in the history of the revelation of his name. In contrast to us moderns, the people of Israel did not consider a person's name as an attribute of chance. Rather the name was designed to express the being of a person. At the same time, it said something about

91

the significance of this person. Knowing another's name implied having a certain power over him or her. Without knowledge of this fact, the account of the revelation of God's name remains incomprehensible. The narrative context within which the revelation of God's name ensues is also important. The Israelites were made the slaves of the Egyptians. When Moses had to witness one of his own people being killed by an overseer, he struck the latter down and fled. One day God appeared to him in a burning thorn bush on Mount Horeb and gave him an order:

"Come, I will send you to Pharaoh and you shall bring my people, the sons of Israel, out of Egypt." But Moses said to God, "Who am I that I should go to Pharaoh, and bring the sons of Israel out of Egypt?" God said, "But I am with you; and this shall be the proof for you, that I have sent you; and when you have brought forth the people out of Egypt, you shall all worship God upon this mountain." Then Moses said to God, "If I go to the people of Israel and tell them 'The God of your fathers has sent me to you,' and they ask me, 'What is his name?' what shall I say to them?" God said to Moses "I am the 'I-am-here.' Say this to the people of Israel 'the I-am-here,' *Yahweh* the God of your fathers, the God of Abraham, the God of Isaac, and the God of Jacob, has sent me to you'. This is my name forever, and thus I am to be remembered throughout all generations." (Ex 3.10-15).

The interpreters of the Bible are all in agreement that God's name, Yahweh, is more a functional than a descriptive name. God promises Moses, and through him the people, the same assistance that he has already given to their fathers—Abraham, Isaac and Jacob—in the past. When God says of himself "I am the 'I-am-here' " he reveals himself as helper and protector in all that may happen. He does not actually say *who he is,* but makes known *how he acts.* In other words he does not emerge from his mystery; but he shows himself to be he who is present with his people. In exposing his name to them, he gives the people no power over him but assures them of his assistance. The images that the prophets use later when they speak of Yahweh-God, reveal that God is to be understood as an opposite, whom one can address. Hosea and Isaiah compare God to a father who inclines towards his son, that is, towards the chosen people (Hos 11.1; Is 63.15 ff; 64.5-7). In the same way the prophets emphasize God's maternalism. Hosea speaks of him as if he were a parent teaching infants to walk. "I took them up in my arms...bent down to them and fed them" (Hos 11.1-4). In Jeremiah God describes his people with motherly prejudice as "my darling child"

(Jer 31.20). When in Deutero-Isaiah the people complain that God has forgotten them, this Lord-God expresses his great tenderness for Israel through the image of wife and mother:

"Can a woman forget her nursing child,
that she should have no compassion
on the son of her womb?" (Is 49.15)

Trito-Isaiah shows how the "Hand of the Lord" reveals itself—like the tender hand of a woman:

"As one whom his mother comforts,
so will I comfort you" (Is 66.13 ff).

Ezekiel, the great prophet of consolation at the time of the exile in Babylon underlines God's solicitousness and power when he calls him a shepherd and a king (Ezek 20.33 ff; 34.11-16). Expressions such as "God of gods" (Ps 136.2) or "Lord of hosts" (Is 6.3) depict God's greatness and magnificence.

Some of the Old Testament presentations of God, however, appear to us today as strange and displeasing. The point at issue here is a God who is subject to passions and outbreaks of wrath. When he sees that the people are turning away from him he says: "I will blot out man whom I have created from the face of the earth, man and beast and creeping things and birds of the air, for I am sorry that I have made them" (Gen 6.7). And he allows the destruction of all humankind with the exception of Noah and his family. Later his words about Saul are in a similar vein: "I repent that I have made Saul king; for he has turned back from following me, and has not obeyed my commandments" (1 Sam 15.11). God can "cry out like a woman in travail, gasp and pant" (Is 42.14). For God—and many parts of the Old Testament proclaim this—is a jealous God whose wrath knows no bounds when his people are unfaithful to him.

It is understandable that modern man has considerable difficulties with an image of God that seems all too close to a depiction of human patterns of behavior. But we must bear in mind that our concept of persons would have been foreign to the people of the Old Testament. Human language about God was the only way to give expression to his personality.

We also have to remember that God revealed himself during the course of a long history. He made his being and his will known step by step. So we should not be astonished if God and his plan of salvation are represented as incomplete and very one-sided in the oldest and earliest sections of the Old Testament. Rather as parents do not try to teach their children everything at once, but according to their intelligence instruct them gradually, God also instructs his people step by step towards an understanding of who he is and what his plans are for them. In theology this is known as a continuous revelation. What is meant by this can be clarified by a comparison. An adult understands his parents better than he did when he was a child. His contact with them has brought him a wealth of experience. Thanks to this experience he is able to understand much that was incomprehensible to him earlier.

This is also the case in the relationship between the chosen people and God. During the course of the centuries they experienced him anew, and consequently the later biblical writers were able to correct a certain bias on the part of the earlier writers. Some points are supplemented in this way, others are relativized. The image and concept of God is perfected during the course of time.

Thus the historical fact of God's self-revelation offers us a key to a better understanding of certain very human statements about him — for example, his wrath or his jealousy. We have to imagine that Israel, after taking over the land in Cana, was confronted with the gods of the local population and with those of neighboring tribes. Initially this polytheism could not be overcome by denying the other gods. It was far more the case of assuming their existence. But it also had to be assumed that Yahweh could prove himself stronger and more powerful than they were. Yet he alone should be honored. The history of religion has called this henotheism. The command: "You shall have no other gods before me" (Ex 20.3) was not primarily directed against belief in the existence of other gods, but simply forbade the worshipping of them. This explains the following: "You shall not bow down to them or serve them; for I the Lord your God am a jealous God..." (Ex 20.5).

The further Israel advanced in its knowledge of God, the clearer it became that its consciousness was being sharpened to accepting that God's jealousy did not represent a base emotion in relation to other gods, but had to be understood from the point of view of his holiness. He is the one God, he alone is holy, and he may not yield up this glory to any other (Is 48.11). He cannot tolerate that his holy name should be profaned. Here the step from henotheism to monotheism is taken. The people of Israel do not worship their God in the way that other peoples worship their gods. Rather, the certainty that there are no other gods gradually prevails. This conviction was generally accepted, at the latest, after the exile in Babylon (586). The change can be followed linguistically. God's holiness came more and more to the fore. The Hebrew word for holiness, *kadosch*, points to what separates and what divides. To the extent that God is experienced as the holy one, he also appears as he who is the other, the only, the sublime over the world. God's holiness includes his transcendence, his eternity beyond this world. He may be experienced as "savior" but he is and remains "the hidden God" (Is 45.15).

In contrast to Christianity, Judaism has no comprehensive teaching on God. It was not until the 12th century that Moses Maimonides summarized the most important beliefs:

1. "I believe with utmost conviction that the creator — praised be his name — has created and guides them and that he alone has accomplished all works, accomplishes and will accomplish them.
2. I believe with utmost conviction that the creator — praised be his name — is one and that no oneness of his is comparable to any relationship and that he alone was, is, and will be our God.
3. I believe with utmost conviction that the creator — praised be his name — has no body and that nothing corporeal adheres to him, and that there is nothing to equal him.
4. I believe with utmost conviction that the creator — praised be his name — is the first and will be the last.
5. I believe with utmost conviction that the creator — praised be his name — alone merits adoration and that it is not seemly to adore any other being except him.
6. I believe with utmost conviction that all words of the prophets are true.
7. I believe with utmost conviction that our teacher Moses is a true prophet and that he is the master of all prophets who were before him and have come after him.
8. I believe with utmost conviction that the Torah as we now possess it, was given to our teacher Moses — may peace be with him.
9. I believe with utmost conviction that this Torah was never exchanged and that no other will come from the creator — praised be his name.

95

10. I believe with the utmost conviction that the creator—praised be his name—knows all the actions of mankind and all its thoughts, so that, 'He who has formed their hearts, all of them, also understands their doings'.

11. I believe with the utmost conviction that the creator—praised be his name—will do good to those who observe his commandments and will punish those who violate his commandments.

12. I believe with the utmost conviction in the appearance of the Messiah and although he has delayed his coming I daily await his arrival.

13. I believe with the utmost conviction that the dead will rise again at a time which will well please the creator. Praised be his name and may his memory be extolled for ever and in all eternity."[5]

These thirteen articles of faith are not teaching formulae but a profession of faith. They are found in the "Siddur," the daily prayer book of the Jews today, and in this way they have gone into the liturgy. However, this profession of faith has never been declared binding for the whole of Judaism.

Apart from the few binding summaries of faith which are concerned with the oneness of God, the revelation of the Torah and the rising of the dead, Judaism knows no dogmas. The Torah itself is not a teaching of faith but an instruction of conduct (Deut 5.1; Amos 5.14 ff; Ps 34.12-15). Judaism is not interested in writings about God but in a life with God. What is demanded is the *emuna*. This concept is usually translated by "faith," but actually rather means trust or loyalty or reliability—or all of them together. The believer experiences God as the Opposite and Thou, he praises and beseeches him, he thanks him, and (one only has to think of Job or Jeremiah!) he quarrels with him. Above all he praises God as the almighty creator, as a powerful liberator, as a true ally. God is the creator of the world (see Gen 2.4-25, an older report; and Gen 1, more recent) and reveals himself within this creation (Wis 13.1-5); he is the liberating and the redeeming God (Deut 26.5-9; Is 44.21-28); he remains faithful to his alliance which he formed with Israel on Mount Sinai (Ex 19-24; 2 Sam 7.8-16); he offers the people a new covenant (Jer 31.32) after the old one was broken because of disloyalty (Jer 22.9; Ezek 16.15-43). The Talmud simply takes God's act of creation for granted. But the creation itself is the theme of numerous discussions and teachings: what was first created, the heavens or the earth (b Chagiga 12a)? During what season did God create the world (b Rosh Hashanah 10b-11a)? When was fire created (b Pesachim 54a)?

The Pesachim tract impressively represents Yahweh as creator, but also as the liberating God:

"In every single generation it is the duty of a human being to consider that it is as if he himself had come out of Egypt, for 'you shall tell your son on that day, it is because of what the Lord did for me that I came out of Egypt' (Ex 13.8). Therefore it is our duty to thank, to praise, to extol, to glorify, to elevate, to bless, to enhance and to render homage to him who performed this miracle for our fathers and for all of us. He led us from thralldom to freedom, out of travail to joy, out of mourning to feasting, out of the darkness into great light, out of slavery to redemption. So we say before him: 'Praise the Lord!' (Ps 113.1)" (b Pesachim X.5).

Like the Old Testament, the Talmud speaks of God not only as the liberator, but also as the God of the covenant, whose loyalty to his word is so great that he even forgets Israel's disloyalty:

"The Holy One, praised be he, spoke: Could I then forget the burnt offerings, the ram and the first-born that you offered before me in the desert? Then they (the community of Israel) said before him: Lord of the world, as there is no forgetting before the throne of your glory—perhaps you also cannot forget the history of the calf (Ex 32)? He spoke to them: Yes, that should be forgotten (Is 49.15). They said before him: Lord of the world, that there could be a forgetting before the throne of thy glory—perhaps you will also forget the history of Sinai (the meeting with God on Sinai is implied; Ex 19-20). He spoke to them: yet I will not forget you (Is 49.15).

"This is what Rabbi Elasar said: Rabbi Oschaja said: what does it mean, that it is written: 'Yes, this should be forgotten'? This refers to the history of the calf. 'But I shall not forget you' refers however, to the story of Sinai" (b Berachot 32b).

Biblical Judaism, like the post-biblical rabbinical tradition, does not indulge in philosophical speculation about God. One speaks about God, and his nearness is experienced. The fact that numerous images of God are used (the forbidding of images in Ex 20.4 is aimed only at the making of graven images!) is as natural as the 'humanizing' of God in concept and language. But images and anthropomorphism do not say anything about God's 'nature.' Instead they are concerned with the relationship between God and man. Such a relationship assumes the

97

knowledge that God, although he lives in heaven (Ps 33.13 ff), is present among his people. In this respect the rabbis speak of the *schechina*, the habitation of God.[6]

The idea of God dwelling among his people originally arose in connection with the sanctum that Yahweh demanded for himself: a gilded ark of acacia wood, in which the tablets of the law were to be kept, and two cherubim placed on the roof, their countenances one to another (see Ex 25.10-22). Invisible over the cherubim, Yahweh was enthroned (1 Sam 4.4), which is why the ark of the covenant was also called "the ark (dwelling) of the Lord" (Josh 3.13). In the end, the nearness of God symbolized by the ark was found to be so intense that the ark of the covenant and God's presence were almost equated with each other. Within the shrine God is almost tangible to his people. It now becomes clearer what the Schechina means — nothing less than *God as he is present to mankind in the shrine, and as he so reveals himself.* Whilst God's "place" is heaven, the place of the Schechina is the shrine. Later the concept of God's dwelling place was gradually transferred to the temple. After its destruction and the displacement of Israel, the Schechina lost its place and became homeless. So Israel's anguish is also God's anguish, because he accompanies his people in all their deprivation. Until the final redemption the Schechina is "present in every praying community, it is among the judges and illuminates their jurisdiction, yes, it is with every individual who learns and prays. So God is not distant from the Jew, but very close to him — one could say that there is a common destiny between God and Israel, and he does not withdraw himself from his people."[7]

Again and again the orthodox Jew asks himself the question; where can God be found? The Hasidic Rabbi Menachem Mendel of Kozk (1783-1859) has given an answer that is worth reflection: "Wherever one invites him to come, he is there."[8]

"In the Name of the Father and of the Son and of the Holy Spirit"

In his teaching Jesus also refers to the God who revealed himself to the people of Israel. All three synoptic gospels bear witness to this. The god of Jesus is the God of Abraham, Isaac and Jacob (Mk 12.26).

Naturally Jesus's consciousness, and therefore all his teaching, are penetrated and stamped by the Old Testament experience of God. For Jesus, God is "not God of the dead, but of the living" (Mk 12.27). He is the creator who cares for his creatures: "Look at the birds of the air: they neither sow nor reap nor gather into barns, and yet your heavenly father feeds them. Are you not of more value than they?" (Mt 6.26). With moving and delightful examples Jesus explains that God's provision does not only apply to the greatest and most extensive things in life but spreads itself over every area: not a sparrow falls to the ground without God willing it. And of human beings who "are of more value than many sparrows" (Mt 10.31)..."but even the hairs of your head are all numbered" (ibid. 30). A person can turn to God in every situation, and does not need "to heap up empty phrases" (Mt 6.7).

Like the Old Testament writers, Jesus in his teaching employs the most varied images when he speaks of God. God appears as the caring father (Lk 15.11-32; Mt 7.9), as the helpful friend (Lk 11. 5-8), as a landowner who rewards everyone more than their services merit (Mt 20.1-16), as a judge whose heart is open to the pleas of the oppressed (Lk 18.1-8).

However, Jesus uses the most daring and revolutionary image of all in the Our Father prayer. Of course God had been described as Israel's father quite early on. The word used for this in Hebrew was *abbinu,* which has a very ceremonial, reverential and distant tone to it. Jesus goes a step further. He does not use the concept *abbinu,* but the trusting, devoted Aramaic expression *abba:* you dear kind father. This is completely new. "There is not one single Jewish text before or at the time of Jesus in which *abba* alone, without any addition, is used as a form of address in prayer."[9]

The Aramaic *abba* comes from the baby language of colloquial children's speech, which was also used when the speaker was no longer a child. It expresses both respect and warmth — we can best translate it into English with the commonplace word "Dad."

Abba — everything is there: sympathy and trust, love and gratitude, affection and warmth, security and tenderness. Of course it is also an image, and this image says: God is not distant but near; he is not cruel but caring; he is not a God without characteristics but a God with passion because he loves human kind passionately.

Abba — naturally it does not mean that we have to imagine God as a masculine being. We have already established that the Old Testament emphasizes his maternal features along with the paternal. It is precisely this image of the motherly father figure that Jesus seizes hold of when he invites us to pray to God as our "Abba." This means he is saying something about human kind at the same time. If God is full of maternal fatherliness towards us, we are no longer his employees or his servants or even his slaves, but his sons and daughters.

It is not that Jesus wishes to trivialize God; he too speaks of God's wrath (Mt 18.34 amongst others). Of course this presupposes that a person does not turn away from God simply out of weakness or in disagreement, but out of pure evil, with knowledge and will.

In his teaching and in his behavior Jesus shows that through him, the relationship between God and man has entered into an entirely new phase. He makes it known that his appearance is combined with a mission which cannot be compared to that of the earlier prophets: "The time is fulfilled, and the kingdom of God is at hand; repent and believe in the gospel" (Mk 1.15).

Jesus teaches that God is well-disposed towards all people. Sinners and the just, the pious and teachers of the Law, customs men and pharisees — all are included within God's love. No one is too humble, no one too sinful, no one too guilty. For God, justice and mercy are not alternatives; rather it is only the justice of mercy which is valid. The parable of the Prodigal Son shows that such an attitude was not unconditionally approved of (Lk 15.11-32); it actually deals with the father's love for *both* of his sons. The father runs to meet the younger and forgives him without reserve; he invites the elder, who remembers his just rewards ("and I never disobeyed your command...") to take part in the feast of reconciliation.

Jesus confirms his teaching about God through his behavior. By sitting together with tax-collectors and sinners, he demonstrates that God makes a new beginning possible for all of us. His love is not dependent on human performance. At the same time Jesus intimates that in his actions he himself manifests God's actions. He links the coming of the Kingdom of God to his own person. One of his statements, whose historicity is generally recognized, points to this: "But if it is by the Spirit of God that *I* cast out demons, then the *kingdom of God* has come upon you" (Mt 12.28). Because the human being Jesus is entirely on the side of God, humanity can meet God in Jesus. This conviction lends expression to the whole New Testament. Only a few examples are necessary. Jesus can do nothing without looking to the father, just as he cannot say who he is without referring to the father (Mt 11.27). The God of Jesus is his father (Rom 15.6; 2 Cor 11.31; Eph 1.3), but Jesus is God's "first born" (Rom 8.29), his "only Son" (Jn 1.14; 3.16, 18). Jesus and the father are so closely bound to each other that in the son one meets the father (Jn 14.9-11). In short, because God himself approaches mankind in Jesus, one can experience in and with Jesus, who and what God is.

An objection seems overdue. Jesus only speaks of the "father." And the Holy Spirit? It is a fact that the Holy Spirit plays almost no part in the preaching of the historical Jesus. On the other hand, all the New Testament authors understand Jesus's life messianically—that God becomes visible in his son. Paul expresses this when he quotes from an early Christian hymn: "He (Jesus Christ) is the image of the invisible God" (Col 1.15). John says the same, when he puts these words into Jesus's mouth; "He who has seen me has seen the father" (Jn 14.9; 8.19; 12.49 etc). After Jesus's death and resurrection the early church takes into account that Jesus is present in her in a new way. This presence is experienced as the working of God's spirit. This spirit is the spirit of Jesus, which works so that his word will be proclaimed further and his work done further. The Acts of the Apostles bear witness to this to such an extent that they have even been described as "The Gospel of the Holy Spirit."

Although the New Testament contains no formulated teaching on the Trinity, we can find the beginnings of considerations which point in this direction; for example, the instructions at the end of Matthew's gospel: "Go therefore and make disciples of all nations, baptizing them in the name of the Father, and of the Son and of the Holy Spirit, teaching them to observe all that I have commanded you" (Mt 28.19 ff). This order from the risen Jesus is formulated by the evangelists according to the practice of baptism, which he had made known to them at the time. Other statements from the New Testament emphasize that the Son as the Word (Logos) has always lived with the Father (Jn 1.1; Phil 2.6); that the coming of the Kingdom of God is connected to Jesus (Mk 1.14 ff); Mt 12.28); that "the Spirit of the Lord" is upon him (Lk 4.18, 21). But the New Testament only says that a relationship between the Father, Son and Holy Spirit exists: the Father sends the Son and the Spirit (Jn 14.16, 26); he sends the Spirit through the Son (Jn 15.26). The New Testament authors show how God has revealed himself as Father, Son and Spirit in the history of human salvation. Theologically this is named the *economic Trinity*. In the New Testament use of language this term "economy" (from the Greek *oikonomía:* administration of resources, careful use of resources) means God's plan (of salvation) and his actions within history (1 Tim 1.4).

However the problem of the *immanent Trinity* had not yet posed itself to the authors of the New Testament, whereby the "inner life" of the Trinity is meant, or more closely, how the relationship between Father, Son and Spirit is to be considered as "inner divine."

By immanent Trinity it is understood what the three-in-one God *is within himself,* whereas the economic Trinity is concerned with how the human being *experiences* God as the three-persons-in-one, as Father, Son and Spirit.

We have unexpectedly stumbled upon the center of Christian doctrine, namely upon the mystery of faith that is the three-persons-in-one God. We have established that this belief has its foundations in the New Testament. From these foundations it was extended and developed during the course of centuries. Later reflection was primarily based on Paul, who as the first theologian, had given systematic thought to the being and workings of the Spirit. Clearly Paul believed that there was only one living and true God (1 Thess 1.9), and one creator (Rom 1.19 ff). Jesus Christ is "the image of the invisible God" (Col 1.15); "For in him the whole fullness of deity dwells bodily" (Col 2.9). Of course there are formulae in Paul which speak only of the Father and the Son: "...yet for us there is one God, the Father, from whom are all things and for whom we exist, and one Lord Jesus Christ..." (1 Cor 8.6). But some of his statements, crystalized from New Testament times, point in the direction of the dogma of the Trinity. The blessing of the apostles on the community of Corinth is known from the liturgy: "The grace of the Lord Jesus Christ and the love of God and the fellowship of the Holy Spirit be with you all" (2 Cor 13.13). Paul introduces his instructions for the Christian life, which he sends to the same community with: "Now there are varieties of gifts, but the same spirit; and there are varieties of service, but the same Lord; and there are varieties of working, but it is the same God who inspires them all in every one" (1 Cor 12.4-6).

Because God has revealed himself to mankind through Jesus, Paul is able to determine the Spirit of God more closely: He is the Spirit of Jesus Christ, of the Son (Rom 8.9; Gal 4.6; Phil 1.19). Paul distinguishes clearly between God, Christ and the Spirit; but as for their activity, the three form a unity: God creates salvation *through* Christ *within* the Spirit.

Similarities occur in the Acts of the Apostles and in John's gospel. In both it is the Spirit who guarantees that the church remains faithful in Jesus's successors: God is present in the church *through* Christ *within* the Spirit.

But how are we to consider the relationship between Father, Son and Spirit? How can one speak of a Trinity within one God, without succumbing to a belief in three gods?

A certain Sabellius (we only know that he came from Libya and was in Rome about 220 AD) attempted to answer this question, in that he depicted the Father, Son and Spirit as *different aspects* of the one God: within himself God is one. The human being however, experiences him in a threefold capacity during the course of the history of salvation and revelation: God, as Law giver, is the Father in the Old Testament, as Redeemer, from birth to ascension, he is the Son, and from then on, he has worked as the Spirit among men. Although Pope Callixtus I expelled Sabellius from the Church, his views found many supporters.

Dionysius, Bishop of Alexandria in the middle of the 3rd century occupied himself with these views, but promptly went to the other extreme. He emphasized the differences between the three divine persons so much, that his opponents accused him of putting forward a belief in three Gods. His namesake in Rome, Pope Dionysius, took part in this argument. The letter that he sent to the Bishop of Alexandria is the first important ruling of the church's teaching body on the mystery of the Holy Trinity. A part of this letter reads:

"One may neither split the admirable and divine unity into three godheads, nor diminish the dignity and the over-powering greatness of the Lord through the expression 'creature.' But one must believe in God, the almighty Father, and in Christ Jesus, his Son, and in the Holy Spirit. (Further one must believe) that the Word (Logos) is united to the God of all things. For he (the Word) says: 'I and the Father are one' (Jn 10.30), and 'I am in the Father and the Father in me' (Jn 14.10). In this way one is aware of both the divine Trinity and the holy teaching of the Monarchy (divine unity)" (NR 249).

But of course this did not dispel the difficulties. New questions were raised when it came to the point of determining the relationship between God and Jesus more closely.[10] This happened at the council of Nicaea (325) which taught the unity of being of the Son with the Father:

"We believe in one God, the almighty Father, creator of all things visible and invisible, and in one Lord Jesus Christ, Son of God, the only one begotten of the Father, that is, out of the being of the Father, God from God, Light from Light, true God from true God....and (we believe) in the Holy Spirit" (NR 155).

The Council says nothing about how the inner life of God should be considered. It simply takes a position against contemporary false teachings, actual or latent. Against a possible interpretation of the Trinity in the sense of a tritheism (a belief in three Gods) it emphasizes the unity of God. Against the opinion that Father, Son and Holy Spirit are simply forms of appearance of the one God, or that the Son is subordinate to the Father (as Arius had taught[11]), the council stresses the divinity of both Son and Spirit, whereby the divine equality of the Son is "explained" by the image of light ("light from light").

As the Council of Nicaea had simply marked out the framework for a doctrine of the Trinity, it was to be expected that theologians would indulge in further speculations on the subject. Three great thinkers "the Cappadocian Fathers," named after their homeland Cappadocia on the northern edge of Syria, were to point the way. They were Basil of Caesarea (c. 330-379), his brother Gregory of Nyssa (c. 334-394) and his friend Gregory of Nazianzus (330-390). Their considerations were to have far reaching effects on the later council decisions.

It was known that the Council of Nicaea had mentioned the Holy Spirit in passing in its confession of faith: "And (we believe) in the Holy Spirit" (NR 155). Arguments about this belief led to violent controversies, in which the Cappadocian Fathers joined. Some people expressed doubts as to the divinity of the Spirit; they saw in him a creature of God or a kind of mediator between God and his creation. Basil and Gregory of Nazianzus on the other hand, pointed out that the Spirit, similar to the Son, proceeded from the Father. To the objection that the Spirit and the Son would then be brothers, Gregory of Nyssa retorted that the Spirit proceeds from the Father *through* the Son. His friend Gregory of Nazianzus clarified the relationship between Father, Son and Spirit through the relationship between Adam, Eve and their son Seth (Gen 4.25): Seth is fathered by Adam and is an equal being with him, Eve however, also an equal being with Adam, has not been fathered by him, but has originated from him: Eve *proceeds from* Adam, but without being fathered by him.

All three Cappadocian Fathers stress the fact that in the end, God is incomprehensible and will remain incomprehensible. This one living God manifests himself within the history of salvation in three strides as it were, as Father, Son and Spirit without ceasing to be a single being. Gradually it was realized that this "outward" revelation of God's must have a counterpart within God himself. If the incomprehensible God announces himself to mankind as a comprehensible Trinity of Father, Son and Spirit, the three are then each characterized by their own "personal" and in this sense not interchangeable attributes: the Father is *unbegotten,* the Son is *begotten,* the Spirit *proceeds from.* Son and Spirit proceed from the Father, but do not leave him. The three therefore do not differ from each other in their being, but purely on the basis of their *proceeding from or not proceeding from.* The *original-being* of the Father, the *being-begotten* of the Son, and the *being-which-proceeds-from* of the Spirit — these three characteristics or individual features divide the one divine being, but not into three independent beings.

In 381 the Council of Constantinople made the teaching of the Cappadocian Fathers its own. The records of this Council have been lost. Research however, has been able to ascertain that the fathers of the Council of Constantinople knew of a confession of faith whose elements tallied with those of the Council of Nicaea. To this the thinking of the Cappadocians was added, and the whole Church was its recipient. In this profession of faith from Nicaea and Constantinople, belief in the divinity of the Holy Spirit was expressly acknowledged: "I believe in the Holy Spirit, the Lord and giver of life, who proceeds from the father (and from the Son).[12] He is adored and glorified together with the Father and the Son. He has spoken through the prophets" (NR 250).

This Credo from Nicaea and Constantinople is still prayed at the celebration of the Eucharist on feast days, and in it the *dogmatic* development of the Christian doctrine of the Trinity has essentially reached its completion. New attetmpts at *theological* interpretations are constantly submitted, and aim to extend the dogma and make it somewhat more comprehensible. That this presents not inconsiderable difficulties is made clear by one single example. Referring to the decisions of the earlier church meetings the second Council of Constantinople summarized the doctrine of the Trinity in a ceremonial decree:

"He who does not profess that Father, Son and Holy Spirit have *one nature or being, one* strength and force; he who does not profess the consubstantial Trinity as *one* godhead which shall be adored as three hypostases or persons, shall be banned (from the church). For there is only *one* God and Father from whom all, *one* Lord Jesus Christ through whom all, and *one* Holy Spirit in whom all, is" (NR 180).

This statement can be traced back to a formula which has marked the common consciousness of faith until our day: there is one God in three persons. Or, to express it in the language of the Council's text, which was Greek: one divine being exists within three "Hypostases." The Greek concept *hypóstasis* (substance, matter, true being) is usually translated into Latin as *persona* (mask, rôle, person, personality) or as *substantia* (being, substance). But when the Greeks were talking about *being* (the being of Jesus or of God) they did not use the word *hypóstasis* but the word *ousía* (essence). This example alone makes us aware of the translation difficulties between the Latin West and the East, where Greek was spoken. But even greater difficulties arise when an expression undergoes a semantic change. This is the case with hypostases/person. (The fact that both expressions do not cover the same meaning need not concern us further).

When we use the concept "person" today, we mean someone with an independent will, consciousness and an awareness of self, with identity and individuality, with a sense of responsibility...If we were to use this concept of person in relation to the Trinity, we would turn the doctrine of the Trinity into a belief in three gods! For within God there is only one will, one strength, one awareness of self, one emphasis of all these....and in this sense (in the sense of our modern understanding of the word person) only one person.

Finally the dogma of the Trinity expresses a fact attested by the scriptures, that God is not a God who reposes within himself, but a God of action, who encounters mankind in three figures. Karl Rahner formulates this:

"This one, incomprehensible God is historically near to mankind in Jesus Christ in an insurpassable way, this Jesus Christ who is not just some prophet in an ever expanding succession of prophets, but the final and insurpassable self-commitment of this one God in history. And this one and the same God shares himself with mankind as the Holy Spirit in the innermost center of human existence, leading to the salvation and perfection which God himself is."[13]

When Christians talk of one God in three "persons" (this is expressly in inverted commas), the concept of person is not used in its actual sense, but as an analogy. Herbert Vorgrimler draws our attention to the results of just such a use of analogy in his "Theological Doctrine of God":

"Proceeding from here, the concept of person in the theology of the Trinity in the sense of the three inner divine relations proves itself to be neither very clear nor very comprehensible. Not for all, but for many theologians, today's theology has again returned to Augustine's pessimistic view of the concepts 'person' and 'hypostases' in the doctrine of the Trinity. Augustine once said that in applying these concepts to the Trinity, their use must be confined to the fact that they make it possible for us to say at least something, instead of having to be satisfied with saying nothing when asked what 'the Three' could be."[14]

Augustine is saying nothing less than that God is—and remains—an absolute mystery. According to Christian understanding, his incomprehensibility is not one characteristic among others, but simply God's attribute of being. God, as the First Vatican Council teaches, is not only "almighty, eternal, immeasurable, incomprehensible, infinite in understanding, in will and in all perfection," but also *"ineffably exalted above all that is outside him and all that can be thought of him."*

Accordingly, God's revelation is not to be understood in the sense that if the "curtain" between him and mankind were simply to be drawn back, he could be perceived in the way in which presents on the Christmas table are perceived when one has removed the wrappings from them. The God that communicates himself does not emerge from the bounds of his mystery; he does not disclose his mystery. It is more that he reveals himself to mankind in his godhead even as he, who he is; as the incomprehensible and unimaginable, as the inexplicable and the ineffable, in short, simply as mystery.

The concept "mystery" has to be understood religiously in this connection, and not colloquially in the sense of "riddle." The latter can be solved, while mystery as such, can only be perceived—in the end it is not at our disposal. For example, we can conceive of someone willingly going to death for another, as Father Maximilian Kolbe did for the father of a family in the concentration camp at Auschwitz. But let us imagine that an unknown person had made up his mind to take such a step. The riddle of his identity could basically be solved. The mystery of the love however, which lies at the center of such a deed, remains. But it is precisely this mystery which can deeply move and affect us. It is the same with the mystery of God. The experience of the great mystics shows us that the more a person becomes immersed in this mystery, the more it moves him and the less he can say about it. He resorts to stammering, he loses himself in wordless amazement and in dumb worship.

And yet the opposite is also true: when one is filled with joy or happiness one simply *has* to speak; so it is with the man who is filled with the blessed mystery of God and feels impelled to speak of it. He is attempting to say what is inexpressible, relying upon images, comparisons or abstract concepts. But because God "remains ineffably exalted above all that is outside him and all that can be thought of him," no image is able to capture his greatness, no comparison can do justice to his being, and no concept can express it appropriately.

But this does not mean that the Christian doctrine of the Trinity was just superfluous speculation. In fact it is an attempt to reconcile the experience of faith conceptually with the God of the Trinity, and to lead the way to this God. Walter Kasper has said, the purpose "of the profession of the Trinity is actually not a teaching about God, but doxology, which is the formula in praise of God."[15] This is most beautifully expressed at the end of the Liturgy of the Eucharist in the Roman rite Mass: "Through him, with him, in him, in the unity of the Holy Spirit, all glory and honor is yours, almighty Father, for ever and ever. Amen."

According to Christian understanding, God is far greater than all that can be thought or said about him. If one has to define God, only this can be said; God is that which cannot be defined. With recourse to the biblical tradition of God, Karl Rahner has repeatedly spoken of the holy and blessed mystery, to which the human being can commit himself in worship and in wonder. The Christian trusts that this holy mystery which he calls God, will bear him up when he falls. In the end, he can only again immerse himself in this mystery.

"There Is No God But Allah"

Not only Jews and Christians, but also Muslims, believe that God revealed himself to mankind in different places, at different times and in many ways. The Islamic conviction that God's announcement of himself is confined to revelation in the Koran may be widespread, but is nevertheless false. The Koran itself expressly and repeatedly points out that God also spoke to man through Abraham, Moses and Jesus. As prophets, these are Muhammad's forerunners, while the Bible to a certain extent represents a distorted version of the Koran. It can only be a version because complete revelation is only contained in the Koran. It is a distorted version because it contradicts the Koran in many respects. Muslims are convinced that the reason for this is that the "owners of the scriptures" (as the Koran describes the Jews and the Christians) falsified the original revelation of Allah; it follows naturally for them then, that different versions of the Bible exist.

From a non-Islamic point of view, the fact that a number of correlations exist between the Bible and the Koran can be otherwise explained; this common ground is the result of encounters — direct and indirect — which the merchant Muhammad had with Christianity and Judaism on his business travels.

However, this is a view that Muslims are unable to adopt. For them the Koran is the unadulterated true word of God, which was communicated to Muhammad through the angel Gabriel (42.52). As the original, personal word of Allah, and the true copy of the original heavenly book (56.77-80), the Koran is an authority that cannot be questioned. Because it originated directly from God, it is superfluous for Muslims to question the cultural, religious and individual assumptions of thought from which Muhammad proceeded.

The revelations which the prophet received cover a period of over twenty years, from about 610, when the forty-year-old experienced his conversion, until 632, the year of his death. This explains why the Koran (Arabic: Qur' an, from qar'a: to read, to recite) is not uniformly structured. It contains exhortations, sermons, instructions, also arguments, confrontations with members of another faith, statutory orders, the teaching of faith and instructions about moral behavior. The individual chapters (Suras) were first collected after the death of the prophet and put together as a whole.

After the Koran, the Sunna (tradition, custom) forms the second chief source of the Islamic religion. It is a transmission, which in practice represents a kind of commentary on the Koran. The literary roots of the Sunna are the Hadithe (singular: Hadit = report): sayings, decrees, stories of the prophet, which were gathered together after his death into a collection of traditions.

The whole faith of the Muslims rests on the Koran and the Sunna, and with it the profession of one single God: "La ilaha illa' llah: there is no other God but God" reads the original and basic form of the faith.

We have already been able to establish that the Islamic conception of God was not uninfluenced by Judaism and Christianity, and why this is so. But early Arabic elements have also left their mark. It is known that Muhammad, who lived from 570-632, only migrated from Mecca to Yathrib, later Medina in 622. This Hidjra (prounounced Hidschra) which means migration or flight, marks the beginning of the Muslim reckoning of time. Therefore the prophet spent the greater part of his life in Mecca, which was seat of the main shrine of the Arabian tribes, the Ka'aba, with the black stone built into it. There Allah, as the highest, but not the only godhead, was worshipped—although the word Allah simply means God.

There had been hermits and seekers after God in Mecca before Muhammad, towards whom the rulers who believed in many gods maintained a sceptical and often dismissive attitude. We do not know whether or to what extent Muhammad's search for God was influenced by them. But it is certain that the teaching that Allah is the one and only God rests both on Arabic sources of faith which had been cleansed of their polytheistic elements, and on statements held to be truths of revelation in both Judaism and Christianity.

The basis of Islam is monotheism. Sura 112 expresses the belief in one and in only one God most succinctly. It represents a kind of shortened form of the Muslim Credo: "Say: God is One, the Eternal God. He begot none, nor was He begotten. None is equal to Him."

A Christian might possibly detect a polemic here against the "begotten not made" in his Credo. But as it is more than likely that this sura originated in Mecca, it was probably directed against the polytheism there, according to which Allah was the father of several daughters. But the Koran teaches that Allah "has taken no wife, nor has he begotten any children" (72.3; 2.116). God creates life through his creative Word, not through the act of begetting in the human sense (2.117). Allah is sufficient unto himself; idols are the gods men serve beside him (27.59). Alone God's greatness speaks against the existence of other gods:

"He who created the heavens and the earth and sends down water from the heavens and causes beautiful gardens to grow. Do whatever you will, you cannot cause such trees to grow. Is there another god with God? Yet there are people who make others equal to Him! He who made the earth, settled and placed it among running rivers and placed firm mountains upon it and placed between the two seas a barrier. Is there another god with God? No, most of them know nothing! He who answers the distressed when they call out to Him and removes the evil. He has given the earth as your inheritance. Is there another god with God? How little of this are you mindful! He who guides you in the darkness, of the land and of the sea and sends winds as signs of his mercy! Is there another god with God? Exalted be He above what they associate with Him! He who began creation and will bring creatures back to life again and gives you provisions from the heaven and the earth! Is there another god with God!'' (27.60-64).

As in the New Testament, blasphemy against the Holy Spirit qualifies as an unforgivable sin (Mk 3.28 ff). According to the Koran, a worshipper of idols finds no forgiveness: "God will not forgive those who serve other gods beside Him; but He will forgive them whom He will for other sins. He that serves other gods beside Him is guilty of a heinous sin" (4.48; 4.116).

The Muslims expressly condemn Christians who, according to their view, pay homage to polytheism. As we have already seen from the portrayal of Jesus in Islam, the Christian dogma of the Trinity is regarded, in the Koran as a belief in three gods. But even if the Trinity had not been interpreted as tritheism, Islam would have had to reject this Christian doctrine. For God is not only the "only one," he is "one-ness" (112.1). While the uniqueness of God's being describes him outwardly, the unity (one-ness) describes his inner life: "God is not only, so to say, outwardly the only one, he is also within himself the one whose being does not divide itself up into several attributes. An inner dividing up of God's being would undeniably lead to an outer division of the godhead itself, that is, to polytheism."[16] Discussions on what is actually meant by the unity in God have led to long and intense arguments within Islamic theology, which we can only deal with briefly here.[17]

The various movements were unanimous as far as the "abstract" attributes of God were concerned: he is without end, eternal, differing from creatures....at the same time the Koran names "positive," "human" characteristics, which concern God's being. Tradition has assembled the ninety-nine "most magnificent names" (7.1 among others).[18] God is merciful, just, powerful; he is the highest, the creator of all things, the nourisher of all things, the judge...because some Muslim theologians were afraid that by naming these attributes and functions of Allah they would split his inner being, they rejected the use of them. Others pointed out that they were taken from the Koran itself. In any case, these attributes do not constitute God's inner being, but simply define it more closely. The question of God has posed highly subtle problems not only to Jewish and Christian theologians (the Schechina, the Trinity), but also to the theologians of Islam!

In the end, the whole discussion revolves around nothing less than the absolute dissimilarity between God and his creation, and therefore around the mystery of his transcendence. Islam, as Judaism and Christianity, emphasizes that God, in his revelation, discloses himself as *simply mystery*. That is why he is "the Visible and the Unseen" (57.3); that is why "nothing can be compared with Him (42.11); that is why in the end "No mortal eyes can see Him" (6.103).

Islamic theology constantly attempts to safeguard God's transcendence. God's most inner being can never be recognized and comprehended by human kind. We only "know" about God that which he wishes to tell us about himself; and so, according to the conviction of many Islamic theologians, the revelation contained in the Koran, in so far as language can ever adequately express the reality of God, also has a part in God's transcendence. We must bear these facts in mind in our brief further discussion of some other aspects of Islamic teaching on God.

(1) The Koran frequently speaks of God as the creator. All—world and mankind, animals and plants, earth and heaven—have to thank him for their existence. He formed heaven and earth out of a solid mass and gave all things life through water (21.30). Some statements are slightly reminiscent of the Bible's account of the creation:

"Say: Do you really misbelieve in Him who created the earth in two days and do you find equals to Him, the Lord of the Universe! He has placed firm mountains above the earth and blessed it and in four days provided food for those who ask. Then he turned to the heaven and it was but vapor and He said to it and to the earth, 'Come, ye two, whether ye will or not!' They said, 'We come willingly!' And in two days He formed seven heavens and assigned each heaven its task. And the lowest heaven he adorned with lamps and guardian angels" (41.9 ff).

"And We did create man from dry clay and mud wrought in form and before this We had created the devils from smokeless fire, and when your Lord said to the angels, 'See, I am creating a mortal from dry clay and black mud. When I have fashioned him and breathed My spirit into him fall down before him in adoration' " (15. 26-29).

"He created the heavens and the earth. He clothes the day with night and the night with day. The sun and the moon are subject to Him and they move by His appointment. He is the Mighty, the Forgiving. He created you from one soul and from that He created its mate" (39. 5-6).

The Koran repeatedly emphasizes that God's Word possesses creative power. "When He decrees a thing, He need only say 'Be' and it is" (2.117).

The early Turkish and Persian miniature artists have given most delightful expression to the high reverence of the Muslims for God's creation. In order to show that nothing was further from them than the wish to surpass God's work, they often added a disturbing or distorted detail to their miniatures.

(2) In so far as God is at work always and everywhere as creator, he is the conserver of the world and of mankind, his providence spreads to all and everything. Allah's work of creation is in no way confined to the beginning. His operative power continues without interruption. This explains why human dealings are sometimes simply ascribed to God. It can happen that the Muslim sees an act of God's creation in the development of natural events, for example in human reproduction:

"We have created man from an extract of clay, then placed him, a clot, in a sure depository (the womb); then We created the clot congealed blood, and We created the congealed blood a morsel; then We created the morsel bone and We clothed the bone with flesh, thus producing another creation. Blessed be God, the greatest of creators!" (23. 12-14).

The second causes which work within creation are therefore not ignored, but refer expressly back to God as the first cause. However, an emphatic distinction between the first and second cause as it is known in Western thought, is no more than an optical illusion for the Muslim. In practice, the problem simply does not arise. God's actions cannot be limited by any causal connections within the world. "Just as God cares for humanity at every moment, so he also holds nature in his hand, and not only as the 'creator'...the world is not clockwork and also does not run its course according to its own laws, but God himself determines every event at every moment."[19] Contrary to all appearances, this does not mean that there is automatically a conflict between faith and knowledge. Islamic thinking also recognizes something like the natural laws, for on the whole God is "not necessarily capricious but" has his customs, and basically, one can rely on these. This is enough for a natural scientist; he knows anyway, that natural laws are nothing other than induced conclusions, that we have to accept as facts until further notice."[20]

(3) God creates life with his creator-Word. But this God does not only have the first word, he also has the last—as "the best of judges" (95.8).

The Koran describes the events at the end of time, particularly the Last Judgement with remarkable detail. Although it depicts the judgement as a terrible and horrifying event, the pious have no need to fear it; for Allah "is the guardian of the faithful" (3.68). It should be pointed out that in this context, faith in God's mercy represents the leitmotif and therefore the criterion of interpretation in the Koran. All the suras (with the exception of the 9th) begin with the introductory formula "In the name of Allah, the Compassionate, the Merciful." The description *ar-Raman,* the Merciful, is so closely linked to Allah that it is really more of a synonym than an attribute.

Faith in one God forms the center of Islam. Tightly knit to this is devoted subordination to his will. This implies the concept of Islam itself, which signifies devotion, the search for peace, or deliverance, and in theological terms is understood as devotion to God. This devotion finds its concrete expression in the fulfilling of the five basic duties laid down by the Koran, which are also described as the "Pillars of Islam." The first pillar is the profession of faith: "There is no God except God and Muhammad is his prophet." This profession of faith is spelled out in more detail in the first sura of the Koran, which at the same time forms the short prayer of the Muslims (and in this sense has a significance for them similar to that of the Lord's Prayer for the Christian):

"Praise be to God, Lord of the worlds!
The Compassionate, the Merciful!
King on the Day of Reckoning!
You alone do we worship,
and to You do we cry for help.

Guide us on the straight path,
The path of those to whom You have been gracious,
With whom You are not angry,
And who go not astray.''

A second basic duty of the faithful is *prayer,* that must be said five times a day, pointing towards Mecca: mornings, afternoons, evenings, at night and at sunrise. On Fridays the Muslims pray together in the mosque led by a prayer leader (Imam). In private and in public prayer obedience to God is expressed by bowing, kneeling and touching the ground with the head. The third main pillar of Islam is *fasting* during the moon month of Ramadan. As the months change according to the moon calendar, Ramadan does not always fall during the same season, so that the abstention from food and drink from daybreak until evening is often linked to considerable sacrifice. The fourth pillar is *the giving* of *alms* (Zakat), or to put it more correctly, social taxes. From the point of view of the faithful, these imply a loan that Allah will reimburse handsomely, rather than a social contribution. The last pillar is the *pilgrimage to Mecca,* (hajj) which every Muslim must undertake at least once in his lifetime, if he is able to.

Naturally there are many other religious regulations known to Muslims, which mark their social and private lives and therefore their relationship to God. As the Koran frequently speaks of reward and punishment in connection with the observance (or non-observance) of these regulations, it is easy to form the impression that Islam is definitely a religion of commandment and forbiddance. Although this opinion is widely held—particularly among members of other faiths—it is not accurate. It is more a case of cause and effect being confused with each other. Because the believer acknowledges God as the one and only, he expresses this acknowledgement in devotional obedience. Reward is not the reason, but the result of his faith. This emerges with moving clarity in a prayer by the Islamic mystic Rabi'a al-Adawiya (c. 717-801):

O my Lord,
When I pray to you
Out of fear of Hell,
I banish myself to Hell.

When I pray to you
Out of hope of Paradise;
I cast myself out of it.

But when I pray to you
For your will's sake,
Let nothing be hidden from me
Of your eternal beauty."[21]

6 Are the Religions Ways to Salvation?

When the subject is religion, most people probably think of religious organizations, of feasts and times marked by religion, of religious duties and institutions. A religion then rests predominantly on shared convictions, rites and ceremonies, in the midst of which individual groups of people ascertain their position in the world and give expression to their hopes and expectations. This is surely a perfectly acceptable description of what we call religion in our daily language. Religion appears then, to be predominantly of social significance.

But this definition does not grasp the essence of religion adequately; its fundamental nature, its quality of transcendence has not been taken into account. Thomas Aquinas refers to this: "Religion is what the worship owed to God provides. Two different things must be considered in religion: firstly, what it brings to God, that is, worship, and secondly, for whom it is provided, namely God."[1] And more concisely: "Religion in its true sense is the relationship to God."[2]

Paul Tillich also uses the concept of relationship in his well-known paraphrase, according to which religion is the relationship to "what implicitly concerns us."[3] To this must be added that we can only truly speak of religion when the relationship to that which implicitly concerns us is positively intended. A blasphemer as a rule has no intention of being religiously active. The same can be said of the person who replaces God with idols. Paul Tillich also takes account of this: "God....is the name for that which unconditionally concerns people. This does not mean that there is at first a being called God, and then the claim that this being should unconditionally concern us. It means that that which unconditionally concerns a person becomes God (or idols), and it means, that only that which is God (or idols) can unconditionally concern him."[4] It follows then, that we can only speak of religion in the theological sense when relationship to God (to what is holy, to our absolutely fundamental perception) expresses itself positively. This implies "that its nature" must be determined "as a redemptive (as seeking redemption and as feeling redemption) relationship" which will provide salvation for the person.

117

No Salvation Outside the Church?

All salvation comes from God. The three great monotheistic religions share this conviction. They also have in common the knowledge of the human need of salvation and the belief that the human being is free to accept or reject this God-given salvation.

Judaism, Christianity and Islam consider themselves to be ways to this salvation. According to how they see themselves and in so far as we are dealing with world religions, they all raise—at least implicitly—a claim to absolutism. Christianity (and after it had divided up, the Catholic Church) has been the most emphatic in this claim. It considered itself to be not only the most perfect religion, but also the one true faith, compulsory for all mankind, the one true way to final salvation:

"The Holy Roman Church...firmly believes, professes and proclaims that no one outside the Catholic Church, neither heathen nor Jew, nor unbeliever nor one separated from the unity will be blessed with eternal life, but will rather fall a victim to the eternal fire which was prepared for the devil and all his angels, if he does not turn to the Church before his death (Mt 25.41)" (DS 1351).

This statement, according to which only members of the Roman Catholic Church can attain final salvation, was made by the council of Florence in 1442. The teaching of one's chance of salvation found in the "Dogmatic Constitution of the Church" (No. 16) from the Second Vatican Council is no less clear:

"Those finally who have not yet received the gospel, are, as a result of this, variously placed in relation to the people of God [the Catholic Church is implied]. First of all comes that people to whom the covenant and the promises were given, and according to whose flesh Christ was born (Rom 9.4-5); that people who are priceless according to his choice and the will of the fathers, and for whom the gifts and calling of God are irrevocable (Rom 11.28-29). But the will of salvation also embraces those who acknowledge the creator, amongst them especially the Muslims, who profess the faith of Abraham and with us pray to the one God, the merciful, who will judge mankind on the last day. But also those others who seek the unknown God in shadows and images, to these also God is not distant, for he gives life and breath and everything to all (Acts 17.25-28), and, as redeemer, wills that all men shall be saved

118

(1 Tim 2.4). Those who through no fault of their own do not know the gospel of Christ and his church, but search for God from honest hearts and strive indeed to fulfill his discernible will at the call of their conscience and under the influence of grace, may attain eternal salvation. Divine providence also does not deny what is necessary to salvation to those, who, through no fault of their own, have not yet come to an express recognition of God, but, not without divine grace, attempt to lead a just life. What is both good and true in them is valued by the Church as preparation for, and as a gift of, the gospel's good news, which enlightens every man, so that he may have life.''

This teaching of the Second Vatican Council stands in direct contradiction to the declaration of the Council of Florence. The latter expressly emphasizes that no one outside the Catholic Church can attain eternal salvation, whereas the Second Vatican Council underlines, also expressly, that not only pagans, Jews and Muslims, but also followers of other religions and even atheists (''those who through no fault of their own, have not yet come to an express recognition of God''), are in no way denied salvation.

The tension which is visible in both these council statements has its basis in the scriptures. Numerous parts of the Bible give the impression that faith and baptism and therefore affiliation to the church represent indispensable requirements for the attainment of salvation. A classical example of this opinion is to be found in the 11th chapter of the Epistle to the Hebrews: ''And without faith it is impossible to please him. For whoever would draw near to God must believe that he exists and that he rewards those who seek him'' (Heb 11.6). As the New Testament understands it, faith means faith in Jesus Christ (Rom 10.9 ff; Acts 4.11 ff). According to John's gospel, baptism as well as faith is a necessary requirement for entry into God's kingdom (Jn 3.5). The demand of the risen Christ in Mark's gospel is also quite clear: ''He who believes and is baptized will be saved; but he who does not believe will be condemned'' (Mk 16.16). The question is, to whom do these statements apply? The verse from Mark shows that salvation is not linked to belief in Jesus Christ and in baptism in an absolute sense; the statement refers to those to whom the good news will be proclaimed, which follows unequivocally from the previous verse: ''Go into all the world and preach the gospel to the whole creation'' (Mk 16.15). The following statement about the condemnation of non-believers can only therefore be valid for those who reject Jesus and his message. It is unnecessary to emphasize that

119

here the evangelist tacitly implies a rejection against his better judgement. A psychological observation about subjective pardonable motives for such a condemnation would have been beyond his horizon. The same can be said of the other New Testament passages mentioned. When the subject is faith (or baptism) as a necessary condition of salvation, then only those people who have already received the word of Jesus are implied (Rom 10.14 ff).

It is therefore not at all surprising that numerous statements are found in the New Testament which emphasize God's all-embracing will to salvation (Tit 2.11; 3.3-6; 1 Tim 2.4). For if God "is the savior of *all men*" (1 Tim 4.10), salvation can in no way be *exclusively* dependent on the answer to faith in the Church's teaching, which can never reach us all.

That salvation is not bound to an explicit profession of faith in Jesus as the Christ in every case, is illustrated in the New Testament by many theological outlines, in which two respective things are carefully differentiated from each other: the fact that the salvation of the world is united to Jesus's work of redemption, and that the fruit of this work of redemption can also act beneficially on those who have not (or not yet) come to know Jesus as redeemer.[6]

No salvation outside the church — this belief of the Council of Florence — becomes a little more understandable when one takes into consideration the conditions and assumptions which caused it. In an age in which the Church was in agreement about expansion with the then known world — America was discovered half a century after the Council of Florence — one could reasonably assume that the gospel had been spread everywhere. Thomas Aquinas for instance, was convinced that heretics and non-believers (Muslims) had had ample opportunity to get to know the Christian faith.[7] If above and beyond this, the rash assumption is made that the truth of the gospels is self-evident, and that any rejection can only be the result of a reprehensible attitude, then one can well maintain that there is no salvation outside the Church.

It was later recognized, although in another context, that the question of salvation could not be reduced simply to the alternatives of being inside or outside the Church. In 1713 Pope Clement XI condemned a number of errors which were found in the main work "Reflexions morales sur les Evangiles" of the French theologian Pasquier Quesnel (1643-1719), among them the sentence: "No grace can be expected outside the Church" (DS 2429). Grace and salvation are now corresponding concepts. Walter Kern observed: "On the one hand one may not say 'Extra Ecclesiam nulla gratia' (there is no grace outside the Church); on the other hand the old axiom 'Extra Ecclesiam nulla salus' (there is no salvation outside the Church) sounds almost the same. This seems to be a prime example of the fact that there is a necessity to amend—not to mention to contradict—official statements of official teaching, which are only really valid precisely within this seemingly conflicting complexity."[8] In 1943 Pope Pius XII attempted to deal with this tension theologically in his encyclical "Mystici corporis." The sentence which states that there is no salvation outside the Church was still adhered to, although the Church's understanding of this was much more comprehensive than it had ever been before. Besides the acknowledged members of the Church, the encyclical recognizes a "figurative" or "latent" affiliation to the Church, in the sense of being placed in a various order of rank to her. All those people who try honestly to follow their conscience and to lead a good life fall into this category. In this sense they are "linked to the Church by a kind of unconscious longing and wish" (DS 3821). This means that the concept "Church" is expanded in such a way that in practice, it embraces all men of good will. Whoever searches for truth, but for some reason or another is not able to recognize it, naturally has the desire for the true Church, and therefore the unconscious wish to belong to it. In so far as he cherishes this unconscious desire, he already belongs to the church, but does not know it. Thus the question of the value of salvation in non-Christian religions can be dealt with easily.

Revelation in the Religions

If grace is able to work in a causal way towards salvation outside the Church, how are the religions affected?

According to the teaching of Thomas Aquinas, the religious practices of pagans are "of no truth or benefit."[9] By the word "pagan" Thomas understands the believing followers of non-Christian religions, with the exception of the Jews.[10] The Second Vatican Council, however, impartially confirms in its "Declaration of the Relationship of the Church to non-Christian Religions," that there is also "truth and holiness" in Hinduism and Buddhism (No. 2), and speaks with "high regard" for Islam (No. 3). Is this truth and holiness simply the result of human mental endeavor, or is it conceivable that non-Christian religions too, in so far as they contain "truth and holiness," could rest—to put it more succinctly—on revelation? From a Christian point of view, there is no doubt about this as far as the Jewish religion is concerned, which is why Thomas makes a distinction between it and pagan religions. The Council declaration expressly calls "the common heritage of Christian and Jew" to mind (No. 4). The same thought is applied to Islam, to the extent that it refers back to the revelation of the Old and New Testaments.

But what is the Council's attitude towards the other religions? In "The Decree on the Church's Missionary Activity" the Council emphasizes, with reference to 1 Tim 2.4-6, that it is God's will that all people shall attain knowledge of the truth:

"So is it necessary that all should be converted to him (Jesus Christ) who is recognized in the teaching of the Church, and to his body, the Church, and shall be integrated through baptism. Christ himself emphasized in express words the necessity of faith and baptism (Mk 16.16; Jn 3.5), thereby strengthening the indispensability of the Church, into which through baptism, the human being enters as if through a door. For this reason a person cannot be saved who knows of the Catholic Church and the necessity of salvation which comes from God and is established in Jesus Christ, but will not enter her or persevere within her (Dogmatic Constitution on the Church, Lumen Gentium No. 14). Although people who do not know the gospel through no fault of their own can be led to the faith by God along paths that are known to him, without this faith it is impossible to please him (Heb 11.6). And so the Church has the obligation (1 Cor 9.16) as well as the sacred right to proclaim the gospel. For this reason missionary activity preserves today and for ever its undiminished importance and indispensability" No. 7).

Our question also finds expression in the "Dogmatic Constitution on the Church" in an important passage (No. 16) which we have already quoted. There it is maintained that God's will to salvation embraces all mankind, so that also those who "through no fault of their own have not yet come to an express recognition of God" but "attempt to lead a just life" can be saved. Another council statement from the "Pastoral Constitution on the Church in the World of Today" is significant here. "As Christ died for all (Rom 8.23) and as in truth there is only one final calling for mankind—the divine—we must stress that the Holy Spirit offers to all the chance to be united to this Easter mystery in a way known to God" (No. 22).

These three texts may complement and interpret each other, but their various statements are not in harmony.

On the one hand the necessity of baptism and membership in the Church are expressly stressed for the attainment of salvation (Missions Decree). On the other hand it is said that God's will to salvation embraces all people (Church Constitution), and that those that do not know the gospel can "also be led by God to the faith along paths that are known to him" (Missions Decree), and that "the Holy Spirit offers the chance to all" to follow their divine calling (Pastoral Constitution).

Again it is said that those "who have not yet received the gospel" are yet within the ranks of the Church "in various ways." But it is also said that this rank cannot be equated with membership in the church, which is necessary for salvation. (Church Constitution).

It is conceded that there is also salvation outside the Church (Missions Decree, Church Constitution, Pastoral Constitution). But the missionary activities of the Church are based upon the impossibility of pleasing God without the faith (Missions Decree).

The Council says that even unbelievers, in so far as they live according to their conscience, are not denied the chance of salvation (Church Constitution). But it also says that there can be no salvation without faith (Missions Decree).

Let us start with this last point in dealing with the problems involved. How can we speak of an indefinite faith in anyone, even in an atheist, who is in need of salvation? The Council has not commented on this question. The Missions Decree simply points to "ways" that "God alone knows" (No. 7). The Pastoral Constitution also says only "that the Holy Spirit offers the chance of faith to all" (No. 22) without explaining how. The question is therefore handed over to theological research.

Karl Rahner above all has provided some helpful considerations. He starts from the position that every person is permanently marked from the beginning by God's grace according to his individual being. This means that although one is able to *distinguish* between a "natural" (purely human) and a "supernatural" (characterized by God's offer of grace) level in mankind, in practice these two levels are not to be separated from each other, as God has always called mankind into communion with him. This "graceful" turning of God towards a person

123

"lifts him up" to the supernatural level from the beginning of his existence. It lies beyond his liberty and knowledge. It does not come to him according to his being (God gives freely of his grace) but in reality imprints itself upon his existence. Rahner describes this human destiny, qualified by grace according to individual existence, as *supernatural existential*. This is to say that at no time in his existence is the human being simply a natural creature, but is called by God to a supernatural salvation. It follows that a person's own experience is always the experience of grace, and therefore the experience of God, whether a person is aware of this or not.[11] And further: if a person takes seriously his responsibility towards himself, towards his fellow human beings and towards society, whether he believes in God or not, he performs an act of grace. For how can he *prove* that it is better to bear his responsibilities rather than to be rid of them? In every case, conscientious behavior presupposes a more or less reflected trust that this behavior has, in the end, some meaning, whereby one manifests anew a basic trust in the reality of the world as a whole.

According to its inner structure such a trust, in its substance, does not differ at all from the faith of a believer, which is also an expression of trust. The faith of a believer is an explicit kind (he knows *whom* he trusts: see 2 Tim 1.12), whilst the trust of a non-believer can be defined as implicit or, to put it in Rahner's terminology, as anonymous.

Such faith however — whether it be implicit or expressly lived — works, according to Christian understanding, for salvation, because in every case it represents an answer to God's obliging gift of grace. When it is said in the Constitution on the Church that "what is good and true" can be seen in someone who has not yet found the God Jesus Christ, and that a "just life" can be led in this case, this happens by virtue of "divine grace" (No. 16). In the "Declaration of the Relationship of the Church to non-Christian Religions" the Council teaches that many of these religions "reveal a ray of that truth which inspires all mankind" (No. 2). Nothing should hinder the Christian from finding an answer to a divine revelation not only in the expressions of faith of followers of other religions but also within these other religions themselves. For God's free communication of himself forms the basis that makes every human response to faith, however inexpressible, possible.

This means that the question of Christianity's claim to absolutism, which rests in the belief in the uniqueness of Jesus Christ, receives a new and broader perspective. The problem, as to which religion now represents the absolute way of salvation, is no longer in the foreground, but the knowledge that religions are indeed ways of salvation. The view that a more open and relaxed dialogue between the religions would be possible on this basis is held by the American theologian Paul M. Knitter in his book "No Other Name?"[12] Knitter emphasizes that previous discussions about the significance of salvation in religions have gone through various stages in Christianity, in that the ecclesiocentric model—no salvation outside the church—has been superseded by the christocentric—Christ as the only savior—which now is being replaced by a theocentric model—God reveals ways of salvation in religions. In this new context he sees the question of Jesus Christ's uniqueness differently:

"Part of this transformative growth will be, I have suggested, a clarification of the theoretical question that has occupied us throughout this book: the uniqueness of Jesus Christ....I have tried to show that it is not necessary for Christians, in their own faith and in their conversation with other believers, to claim the "finality" or "normativity" of Jesus. But I also added that, though such a claim, at the present stage of interreligious encounter, need not and cannot be made, it may still be true. Perhaps something has happened in the historical event of Jesus Christ that surprisingly surpasses all other events. Perhaps God's historical revelation in Jesus—limited and relative like all history—contains and explains all other relative historical revelations. Perhaps what took place in the history of Jesus goes beyond anything found in the collective unconscious and myths of humankind."[13]

The question is however, whether a bare "perhaps" is enough for the Christian to profess faith in the resurrection, or whether this profession can only be answered when it rests upon an inner certainty. On the other hand, it must be considered that both Judaism and Islam hold that God wills the perfection, and so the salvation, of all mankind.

If God offers all mankind the chance of salvation, it means that this salvation cannot be attained in reality directly through the religions, but that the path of conscience and the ethical dimension of experience are "to be defined theologically as the place where salvation is determined and as the substance of ways to salvation."[14] In this respect the question of Jesus Christ's uniqueness is indeed relativized. But this does not imply that the question of truth is left to the choice of the individual, in the sense that anyone can find his own salvation.

Everyone is responsible before his conscience to seek the truth, not to close his eyes to it, and then act in accordance with the insight he has gained.

If the Christian will hold fast to the uniqueness of the way of salvation preached and practised by Jesus, and profess himself to Jesus Christ as the literal way to salvation, it does not mean that he has to break off dialogue with other religions. His faith, too, represents a lifelong process. This also implies though, that he has to re-analyse and recheck his commitment to this faith. Here, too, Knitter's "perhaps" is justifiable.

The fact that followers of other religions are not excluded from salvation has not been without consequences for missions: even if they can no longer be understood simply as a kind of "salvation business" with a view to the hereafter, they still remain:

"...a valid, meaningful concern. But it is no longer the primary goal, the *raison d'être,* of missionary endeavors. If others are converted to the Christian community, the missioner will rejoice, as long as the conversion has taken place freely and as an integration of the person's personal-cultural identity. But if conversion to Christianity does not take place, the missionary's spirit need not wilt. The central purpose of mission is being realized as long as, through mutual witnessing, all are converted to a deeper grasp and following of God's truth."[15]

This implies that the Christian also affirms that followers of other religions should observe their responsibilities, and pursue the aims of these religions in accordance with their conviction. Mission occurs in and as dialogue, which rests upon "personal religious experience" and "must be grounded in the hypotheses of a common ground and goal for all religions."[16]

Knitter names three necessary criteria for such a dialogue:
"1) *Personally,* does the revelation of the religion or religious figure—the story, the myth, the message—move the human heart? Does it stir one's feelings, the depths of one's unconscious?
2) *Intellectually,* does the revelation also satisfy and expand the mind? Is it intellectually coherent? Does it broaden one's horizons of understanding?
3) *Practically,* does the message promote the psychological health of individuals, their sense of value, purpose, freedom? Especially, does it promote the welfare, the liberation, of all peoples, integrating individual persons and nations into a larger community?"[17]

These criteria are far more of a practical than a theological nature. They are applicable to the three great monotheistic religions — but history shows that each of these religions does not comply with them all the time to the same extent, but only approximately.

And each of these religions, according to how its followers see it, is the — or a — way which leads to God and therefore to salvation. The differences are essentially concerned with this way of salvation and are therefore of a didactic nature. There is agreement as to the *goal* that the human being should attain. But many basic religious experiences are also related, which implies that the followers of each of these three religions should take the other professions of faith seriously as answers to faith. Finally, they are to be taken seriously because Muhammad knew, to the same extent that Jesus and Moses knew, that he was called by God, and because the message of each of these three figures is a deep experience of God.

Judaism, Christianity and Islam never approach each other so closely as when their followers abandon themselves completely to the mystery of God and entrust themselves to him, as in mysticism. The prayers of the mystics make this abundantly clear.

"O God, put Light into my heart, Light into my ears,
Into my eyes Light and into my tongue Light;
Light to my right and Light to my left;
Light above me and Light beneath me;
Light before me and Light behind me!
Put Light into my soul!
Make the Light great for me!
Widen my breast, and make my task easy! O God, thou hearest my words and thou seest my sojourn. Thou knowest my secret and my revealed works, and nothing of my life is hidden from thee.
I am desolate and poor, I cry to thee for help and assistance, in fear and in anxiety I confess and admit my guilt.
I beg thee as a wretch begs; I implore thee, as one who is debased; I cry to thee as the fearful blind man cries, who bends his neck before thee, whose tears flow before thee, and whose body demeans itself before thee, and whose pride is humbled before thee."

"I will extol thee, my God and
King,
and bless thy name for ever and ever.
Every day I will bless thee,
and praise thy name for ever and ever.
Great is the LORD and greatly to be praised,
and his greatness is unsearchable.
One generation shall praise thy works
to another,
and shall declare thy mighty acts.
I will speak of the glorious honor of thy
majesty
and of thy wondrous works.
Men shall speak of the might of thy
terrible acts,
and I will declare thy greatness.
They shall abundantly utter the memory of thy
great goodness,
and shall sing of thy righteousness."

"O flame of the living love, which has pierced my innermost soul!
Canst thou not cease from endless complaining? Accomplish it then!
Accomplish it! Tear apart the decayed tissues, the last remains that
thrust themselves between him and me.
The fire refines, the sword severs! O desired fire, longed for wounds!
Whose is the gentle hand that mitigates all pain? The perfumes of
Eden stream from it.
It effaces all guilt—it heals the dying, and for death it gives life.

You flaming torches, in whose summer brilliance the darkest grottoes
shine again—
He was blind and encompassed by night, but his darkness was
transfigured by light,
And the dead ashes burst into blazing fire!
I feel him stirring within my innermost parts, the gentle, the friendly,
who has never abandoned me.

I feel him, I taste him, I feel the travail of his breath, Glory radiates
above me; blessedness surrounds me. Overwhelmed with joy, I perish
in love!"

Which prayer can be ascribed to which religion? Could not the first, which Islamic tradition ascribes to Muhammad, come from St John of the Cross (1542-1591), the author of the third? And could not Christians and Muslims pray to God together with the author of the second—of Psalm 145?[18]

But to avoid misunderstandings: the differences in teaching between the individual religions are certainly not without significance. They achieve results which often extend far beyond the private realm into social and political life—one only has to think of the Jewish interpretation of the promised land, of the Christian theories of a just war, of the administration of Islamic legal maxims...But as long as the religions (inwardly and outwardly) predominantly quarrel about differences in teaching, religion as such has no future. Mysticism has been spared this kind of confrontation because it does not proceed from theory, but from contemplation of the mystery of God, and exists from the experience arising out of this, which represents the aim of all religions. Is the thought illusory, that the experience of God common to the religions could, more than anything else, contribute to a more sober evaluation of the differences in teaching, to support these in a more relaxed way; and perhaps, at least to some extent, to reconcile them? And does not every religion which makes the mystical experience possible, herald salvation for those who have this experience?

To whom does Jesus belong? At the end of our deliberations, there is only one possible answer to the question: Jesus belongs to all because he allows all human beings to share in his experience of God. But to this we must add: Moses and Muhammad belong to all as well. Which means that each of these three great figures possesses an additional significance for those people who turn to them in a particular manner. Ultimately though, all three desired one thing: to show the way to God, and therefore to salvation.

Notes

From Polemic to Dialogue

1   See "Sources" for quotations from official Church documents.
2   Patrologia latina 87, 952-954; in G. Bachl, "über den Tod und das Leben danach", (Graz, Vienna, Cologne 1980), pp. 219-221. Further examples given there.
3   Compare the Definition of Heresy in can. 751 of Church Law: "Heresy is that *persistent* (pertinax) denial ensuing after baptism, of a truth to be believed according to the divine Catholic faith, or a *persistent* doubting of such a truth" (italics are mine).
4   Compare F. Mußner, "Traktat über die Juden", (Munich 1979), pp. 212-241 with the following.
5   Mußner, pp. 309-310.
6   H. Küng, "Die Kirche" ("ökumenische Forschungen, Ekklesiologische Abteilung" vol. 1) (Freiburg Basle Vienna 1967), p. 165 ff.
7   For the foundations of such a discussion compare Küng pp. 167-180.
8   "Nova agendi ratio", in "Acta Apostolicae Sedis", 63, (1971) pp. 234-236.
9   Dostoevsky expresses these circumstances in relation to the prisoner Christ who has returned: "You did not come down from the cross, when mocking and scoffing at you, they called out 'Come down from the cross and we will believe that you are he!' But you did not come down because you did not want to enslave man anew through a miracle, because you yearn for his free faith and not for faith in miracles. You yearn for love in freedom and not for the servile enthusiasm of a slave in the face of a power which has struck terror into him once and for all." F. M. Dostoevsky "The Brothers Karamazov" — translated from the German Winkler edition (Munich 1958 p. 345) by the translator.
10 Compare "Dignitatis humanae", No. 9, Note 8.
11 Thomas Aquinas, "De veritate", 17, 4, ad. 1.
12 This applies, however, only to the Jews and unbelievers. Thomas does not exclude the use of force against heretics; compare "Summa theologica", II-II, 10.8; 11.13.
13 Thomas Aquinas, "Summa theologica", II-II, 10.11.
14 Compare DS 3165-3179.

1   Quoted from: Shalom Ben-Chorin, "Bruder Jesus. Der Nazarener aus jüdischer Sicht" (dtv vol. 1253, Munich (ix) 1986), p. 10.
2   P. Lapide. "Ist das nicht Joseph's Sohn? Jesus im heutigen Judentum" (Gütersloher Taschenbücher vol. 1408) Gütersloh, 1983, p. 42.
3   For the placing of Jesus in Judaism, compare also: W. P. Eckert, "Jesus und das heutige Judentum" in: F. J. Schierse (Ed), "Jesus von Nazareth", (Mainz 1972); R. Gradwohl, "Das neue Jesus-Verständnis bei jüdischen Denkern der Gegenwart", in: Freiburger Zeitschrift für Philosophie und Theologie 20 (1973) pp. 306-323; W. Dantine, "Jesus von Nazareth in der gegenwärtigen Diskussion", (Gütersloh 1974); H. G. Pohlmann, "Wer war Jesus von Nazareth?" (Gütersloh (ii) 1977); H. Freis, "Jesus in jüdischer Sicht", in H. Fries/F. Köster/F. Wolfinger (Ed), "Jesus in den Weltreligionen", (St Ottilien 1981), pp. 15-49; F. König/E. L. Ehrlich, "Juden und Christen haben eine Zukunft", (Zürich 1988); esp. pp. 135-141.
4   The Talmud: for contents, structure and manner of quotation see "Sources" at the end of this book. Compare also: J. Maier, "Jesus von Nazareth in der talmudischen überlieferung" (Erträge der Forschung, vol. 82) (Darmstadt 1978).
5   Examples in: A. Th. Khoury (Ed), "Lexikon religiöser Grundbegriffe. Judentum Christentum Islam", (Graz, Vienna, Cologne 1987), p. 529.
6   Mendelssohn: cit. Khoury, p. 530; Lapide, p. 87; Ben-Chorin, p. 186.
7   The following representation of the rabbis is largely based on Lapide, pp. 81-167.
8   Mose Maimonides, "Mischne Tora, Hilchot Melachim" XI, 4; cit. Lapide, 104.
9   Sa'd Ibn Mansur Ibn Kammuna, "Erforschung der drei religionen"; cit. Lapide, p. 102 ff.
10 Compare Lapide, p. 107.
11 cit. Lapide, pp. 115, 116.
12 M. Mendelsohn, "Jerusalem", (Leipzig 1843), p. 357.
13 Compare M. De Jonge, "Jeschua, der klassische jüdische Mann. Zerstörung des kirchlichen, Enthüllung des jüdischen Jesusbildes", (Berlin 1904), p. 100: "Out of the gospel, you Holy Joes! Hands off Jeshua! Give over your prey! Jeshua for the Jews!" (cit. Lapide, p. 122; further evidence of the then growing interest of the Jews in Jesus: Ibid., pp. 123-140)
14 H. G. Enelow, "A Jewish View of Jesus", (New York 1920), p. 181; cit. Lapide, 133.
15 Enelow, p. 166.
16 J. Klausner, "Jeschu Ha-notzri", (Jerusalem 1922); Engl: 1925; Ger: "Jesus von Nazareth. Seine Zeit, sein Leben und seine Lehre", (Berlin 1930).

17 Ibid. (ii) 1934, p. 574.
18 L. Baeck, "Das Evangelium als Urkunde der jüdischen Glaubensgeschichte", (Berlin 1938), p. 30.
19 Ibid. p. 70.
20 Ibid., p. 69 ff.
21 M. Buber, "Zwei Glaubensweisen", (Zürich 1950; reprinted in: Werke, vol. 1, Munich, Heidelberg, 1962), pp. 652-782; 657)
22 Ben-Chorin (Note i), p. 11. In the following quotation page references are given in brackets. Compare Th. Pröpper's critical analysis, "Der Jesus der Philosophen und der Jesus des Glaubens" (Mainz 1976) pp. 70-94.
23 Shalom Ben-Chorin, "Jesus im Judentum," (Wuppertal, 1970), p. 67.
24 P. Lapide, "Der Rabbi von Nazareth" (Trier, 1974) "Juden und Christen" (Zürich, Einsiedeln, Cologne 1976); "Auferstehung. Ein jüdisches Glaubenbekenntnis", (Stuttgart, Munich, 1977); H. Küng, P. Lapide, "Jesus im Widerstreit, Ein jüdisch-christlicher Dialog", (Stuttgart, Munich, 1976); P. Lapide/J. Moltmann, "Jüdischer Monotheismus—Christliche Trinitätslehre. Ein Gespräch" (Munich, 1979); P. Lapide/C. F. von Weizsäcker, "Die Seligpreisungen. Ein Glaubensgespräch (Stuttgart, Munich, 1980); P. Lapide/K. Rahner, "Heil von den Juden? Ein Gespräch" (Mainz, 1983). Quotations from these works follow under abbreviated titles and the page numbers are in brackets.
25 D. Flusser, "Jesus in Selbstzeugnissen und Bilddokumenten" (Reinbek, 1968); compare Dantine (note ii) pp. 38-41.
26 H. Fries, "Zietgenössische Grundtypen nichtchristlicher Jesusdeutungen" in: L. Scheffczyk (Ed.), "Grundfragen der Christologie heute" (= Quaestiones disputatae Vol. 72), (Freiburg, 1975), pp. 36-76, 69.
27 "Declaration of the Relationship of the Church to non-Christian Religions", Nostra aetate, No. 4.
28 Lapide, "Ist das nicht Josephs Sohn"? (Note 2) pp. 47-80.
29 P. Navé, "Die neue hebräische Literatur", (Bern, 1962), p. 96; compare Lapide's opinion in "Ist das nicht Josephs Sohn?" p. 38: "Clearly the best novel about Jesus in Hebrew literature."
30 cit. Lapide, "Ist das nicht Josephs Sohn?" p. 42. In the first chapter "Jesus in der hebräischen Literatur" the author draws attention to some further examples (short stories, ballads, novellas) in which Jesus is more or less the subject.
31 H. Domin, "Ecce Homo" in "Ich will Dich." Poems, (Munich, 1970), p. 19. Literary examples of Jewish approaches to Jesus can be found in K. J. Kuschel (Ed) "Der andere Jesus. Ein Lesebuch moderner literarischer Texte." (Zürich, Einsiedeln, Cologne/Gütersloh, 1983), pp. 351-386.
32 F. Mußner, "Traktat über die Juden", (Munich, 1979), pp. 310-335, 310. Quotations which follow have page numbers in brackets.
33 F. Rosenzweig "Letters", (Berlin, 1935), p. 73.

Son of Man and Son of God: Jesus in Christianity

1   Many further references to this subject: H. Frankemölle,
    "Glaubensbekenntnisse". Zur neutestamentlichen Begründung unseres
    Credos", (Düsseldorf, 1974); W. Kasper, "Jesus der Christus",
    (Mainz 1974); F. J. Schierse, "Christologie", (Düsseldorf, 1979); T.
    Schneider, "Was wir glauben. Auselgung des Apostolischen
    Glaubensbekenntnisses", (Düsseldorf, 1985): W. Simonis, "Jesus von
    Nazareth. Seine Botschaft vom Reich Gottes und der Glaube der
    Urgemeinde" (Düsseldorf, 1985).

2   The Hebrew Almáh in the meantime implies a young woman who
    need not necessarily be a virgin—the German Ecumenical translation
    of the Bible draws attention to this in a footnote to Is 7.14.

3   The origin of belief in Easter; compare J. Imbach "Himmelsglaube
    und Höllenangst. Was wissen wir vom Leben nach dem Tod?"
    (Munich, 1987), pp. 97-107.

4   Compare Tacitus (c. 55-116) "Annals" 15, p. 4; Suetonius (c. 70
    A.D.) "Life of Claudius", p. 25; Pliny the Younger (c A.D.
    61/62-113) "Epistola, 10, p. 69; Joseph Flavius (37/38—c. 100)
    "Judische Altertümer, 20, p. 200.

5   Further details: J. Imbach, "Die Bibel lesen und verstehen", (Munich
    1986), pp. 120-146.

6   Simonis gives many details about dating, pp. 204-208.

7   Simonis, p. 233.

8   Compare R. Pesch, "Wie Jesus das Abendmahl hielt" (Freiburg,
    1977).

9   A detailed and generally comprehensible view can be found in R. P.
    McBrien, "Was Katholiken glauben" vol. 1, (Graz, Vienna, Cologne,
    1982), pp. 309-402; also compare Schneider (Note 1), pp. 220-231.

10 Letters to the Trallians, 9.

11 The following brief view of the representation of Christ in art is partly
    analogous, partly taken from H. Küng, "Christsein", (Munich, 1974),
    p. 120.

12 Further information in chapter 5 of this book.

13 K. Rahner/K. H. Weger, "Was sollen wir noch glauben?" (Freiburg i.
    Br. 1979), p. 121

14 Ibid., 115.

Allah's Apostle and Envoy: Jesus in Islam

1   For the understanding of Jesus in the Koran and in Islam, compare G.
    C. Anawati, "Isa", in Encyclopédie de l'Islam, Tome 4,
    (Leiden/Paris, 1978) pp. 85-90 (Lit.); F. Köster, "Jesus in Islam" in:

H. Fries/F. Köster/F. Wolfinger (Ed.), "Jesus in den Weltreligionen", (St. Ottilien, 1981) pp. 51-76; K. Samir, "Cristo nel Corano" in: "La Civiltà Cattolica 134", (1982 II), pp. 450-462; the same; "Teologia coranica di Cristo" in: Ibid., pp. 556-564; A. Th. Koury (Ed.), "Lexikon religiöser Grundbegriffe. Judentum Christentum Islam" (Graz Vienna Cologne, 1987) pp. 542-546 (Lit.).

2   Compare the Protoevangelium of James, 5.2 (birth of Mary); 8.1 (feeding of Mary "from the hand of an angel"); Pseudo-Gospel of Matthew 4.6, 3. Ger. translation in E. Hennecke, "Neutestamentliche Apokryphen" 3. New version ed. by W. Schneemelcher, Bd. 1: Evangelien (Tübingen, 1959)

2   Compare Anawati, p. 85.

4   Eirenaios of Lyon, "Adversus Haereses", I, 24.4.

5   C. Schedl. "Muhammad und Jesus. Die christologisch relevanten Texte des Koran". (Vienna, 1978) p. 469 ff.

6   Compare A. Th. Khoury, "Begegnung mit dem Islam", (Freiburg, Basle, Vienna, 1980) p. 44.

7   Compare M. Eliade, "Geschichte der religiösen Ideen" vols. III/I, (Freiburg, Basle, Vienna, 1983) p. 83.

8   Compare Anawati, p. 87.

9   Khoury, Lexikon (note i,) p. 544.

10 Compare G. C. Anawati, "Polémique, apologie et dialogue islamo-chrétiens" in: "Euntes docete" 22 (1969) pp. 375-451.

11 To the following: Ibid., pp. 380-392.

12 Compare G. Rizzardi, "Maometto-anticristo nei commentari dell'Apocalisse" in: "Renovatio" 12 (1987) pp. 57-87.

13 Compare Anawati, "Encyclopédie", p. 89; "Polémique", p. 450.

14 J. van Ess, "Jesus im Koran". "Islamische Perspektiven" in: H. Küng/J. van Ess/H. von Stietencron/H. Bechert, "Christentum und Weltreligionen", (Munich Zürich, 1984) pp. 157-172; 159.

15 P. Rondot, "Der Islam" cit. Köster, (note i), p. 66.

Who Is God?

1   M. Buber, "Gottesfinsternis" in: Werke, vol. 1. (Munich, 1962) p. 509.

2   K. Rahner, "Grundkurs des Glaubens", (Freiburg, Basle, Vienna, 1976), p. 56.

3   P. Lapide, "Gott im Judentum", in: A. Th. Khoury/P. Hünermann (Ed.), "Wer ist Gott? Die Antwort der Weltreligionen", (Freiburg, Basle, Vienna, 1983) pp. 53-72; 56.

4   N. Lohfink, "Gott. Polytheistisches und monotheistisches Sprechen von Gott im Alten Testament" in: "Unsere großen Wörter. Das alte Testament zu Themen dieser Jahre", (Freiburg, Basle, Vienna, 1977),

pp. 127-144; see also A. Deissler, "Die Grundbotschaft des Alten Testaments. Ein theologischer Durchblick", (Freiburg, Basle, Vienna, 1972))

5   Mose Maimonides, "Kommentar zur Mischna, Traktat Sanhedrin": cit. P. Meinhold, "Die Religionen der Gegenwart" (Freiburg, Basle, Vienna, 1978) p. 215 ff.

6   In the following I refer to A. M. Goldberg, "Judentum" in E. Bruner-Traut, (Ed.), "Die fünf großen Weltreligionen" (Freiburg, Basle, Vienna (xiii) 1985), pp. 88-106; esp. 93 ff. Also see A. Th. Khoury (Ed.), "Lexikon religiöser Grundbegriffe. Judentum Christentum Islam", (Graz, Vienna, Cologne, 1987) p. 409 ff.

7   Goldberg, p. 94.

8   P. Kuhn (Ed.), "Weißt du, wo Gott zu finden ist? Geschichten aus dem chassidischen Judentum" (Kevalaer, 1984), p. 10.

9   O. Knoch, "Jesus—Beter und Lehrer des Gebets" in: Sh. Ben-Chorin/P. Kaczynski/O. Knoch, "Das Gebet bei Juden und Christen" (Regensburg, 1982) pp. 27-51; 38 ff.

10 Compare the chapter "Son of Man and Son of God: Jesus in Christianity" in this book.

11 For the relationship between God and Jesus, see the chapter mentioned in note 10.

12 "And from the Son" (in Latin *Filioque*) was first added to the Credo in Spain in the 6th century. In Rome it was officially added in 1014. The Eastern Church rejected the "Filioque" from the beginning.

13 K. Rahner, "Einzigkeit und Dreifaltigkeit Gottes im Gespräch mit dem Islam" in: "Schriften zur Theologie" vol. 13, (Zürich, Einsiedeln, Cologne, 1978) pp. 129-147; 139 ff.

14 H. Vorgrimler, "Theologische Gotteslehre", (Düsseldorf, 1985), p. 128.

15 W. Kasper, "Der Gott Jesu Christi", (Mainz, 1982), p. 370.

16 A. Th. Khoury, "Wer ist Gott für den gläubigen Muslim?" in: A. Th. Khoury/P. Hünermann (Ed.) "Wer ist Gott? Die Antwort der Weltreligionen" (Freiburg, Basle, Vienna, 1983) pp. 73-91; 88.

17 Further in L. Gardet, "Allah" in: Encyclopédie de l'Islam, (Nouvelle édition, tome I, Leyde Paris, 1960), pp. 418-429 (Lit.).

18 For the name of Allah, see L. Gardet, "al-asma" in Ibid., pp. 735-739.

19 J. van Ess, "Gottesbild und islamische Mystik, Menschenbild und Gesellschaft" in: H. Küng/J. van Ess/H. van Stietencrown/H. Bechert, "Christentum und Weltreligionen" (Munich, 1984) pp. 119-136; 124.

21 Ibid., p. 125.

21 Cit. after G. Bachl, "über den Tod und das Leben danach", (Graz, Vienna, Cologne, 1980), p. 198.

1 Thomas Aquinas, "Summa theologica", II-II, 122.2.
2 Ibid., II-II, 81.1.
3 P. Tillich, "Systematische Theologie" vol. I., (Stuttgart, 1956), p. 247.
4 Ibid.
5 M. Seckler, "Der theologische Begriff der Religion" in: W. Kern/H. J. Pottmeyer/M. Seckler (Ed.), "Handbuch der Fundamentaltheologie" vol. I: Traktat Religion (Freiburg, Basle, Vienna, 1985), pp. 173-194; 182.
6 Compare G. Lohfink, "Universalität und Exklusivität des Heils im Neuen Testament" in: W. Kasper (Ed.), "Absolutheit des Christentums (Quaestiones disputatae, Vol. 79), (Freiburg, Basle, Vienna, 1977) pp. 63-82.
7 Thomas Aquinas, "Summa contra Gentiles", 1, 6.
8 W. Kern. "Außerhalb der Kirche kein Heil?" (Freiburg, Bssle, Vienna, 1979) p. 48 ff.
9 Thomas Aquinas, "Summa theologica", II-II, 10, 11.
10 Ibid., II-II, 10, 5.
11 See K. Rahner, "Anonymer und expliziter Glaube" in: "Schriften zur Theologie" vol. 12, (Einsiedeln, Zürich, Cologne, 1975), pp. 76-84.
12 P. F. Knitter, "No Other Name?—a Critical Survey of Christian Attitudes toward the World Religions" (New York, 1985).
13 Ibid., p. 230.
14 M. Seckler, "Theologie der Religionen mit Fragezeichen" in: Theologische Quartalschrift 166 (1987) pp. 164-84; 179.
15 Knitter, p. 222.
16 Ibid., p. 207, 208.
17 Ibid., p. 231.
18 Muhammad's prayer in: "Mohammed für Christen" (Introduction: Muhammad Salim Abdullah. Texts chosen by A. Th. Khoury), Freiburg i Breisgau, 1984) p. 183 ff; Psalm 145, 1-8; St John of the Cross, "Lebendige Liebesflamme" in C. Einiger (Ed.) "Die schönsten Gebete der Welt" (Munich, 1964), p. 72. English translations of Muhammad's prayer and the prayer of St John of the Cross by the translator of this book.

Sources, Abbreviations

The Bible

The author has quoted from the "Einheitsübersetzung: Die Bibel. Altes und Neues Testament." Edition commissioned by the Bishops of Germany, Austria, Switzerland, the Bishop of Luxembourg, the Bishop of Liège, and the Bishop of Bolzano-Brixen. The Psalms and the New Testament were also commissioned by the Council of the Evangelical Church in Germany and the Evangelical Bible Studies of the then Federal Republic of Germany.

The Talmud

The Talmud (literally, the Study) is a collection of laws and religious records of post-biblical Judaism, which developed during the time c. 200 B.C. to roughly 500 A.D. In the outer form of the text one distinguishes between the *Mishnah* ("repetition," which is the teaching of the fathers, learnt by being repeated sentence by sentence), and the *Gemara* (completion of the teaching or commentaries by later teachers). The inner form of the Talmud, however, divides into the *Halacha* and the *Haggada*. The Halacha (way of life) contains the laws—guides, decisions of the masters, the passing on of traditional customs—and takes up about two thirds of the book. The Haggada (narration) includes narrative collections, i.e. proverbs, parables, legends, anecdotes. The whole Talmud consists of six main portions or rules (agriculture, feast times, marriage law, civil and criminal law, holy objects, ritual cleansing instructions), which in their turn are divided into single tracts.

There are two versions of the Talmud named according to their place of origin: the Palestinian (Jerusalem) and the Babylonian Talmud—when speaking simply of the Talmud, the latter more comprehensive version is usually implied.

As a rule the author quotes from R. Mayer: "Der Talmud," Goldmann Verlag, (Munich (viii) 1986). Translations into English in this book are by the translator.

Notes on the translations: a *b* or a *j* signifies the Babylonian or Palestinian (Jerusalem) Talmud. Quotations from Mishnah have Roman numerals to signify their chapters, and Arabic numerals to mark the paragraphs. The Gemara is quoted according to sheet and page, the *a* signifying the facing page, the *b* the reverse page.
Ex:
j Chagiga II.2: Palestine Talmud, tract Chagiga (= ceremonial offering), Mishnah, ch. 2. par. 2.

b Sanhedrin 43a; Babylonian Talmud, tract Sanhedrin (= law court), Gemara, p. 43, facing page.

The Koran

The sacred text of the Muslims is the Koran. According to Islamic belief, this is a faithful copy of the primal Heavenly Book, which was revealed to Muhammad during the years 610 to 632—the year of his death. Qur'an (from qar'a = reading, recital) literally means "that which has to be read often" (book). The Koran consists of 114 Suras (chapters) which, similar to the books of the Bible, are subdivided into verses. With the exception of the 9th, all the Suras begin with the introductory formula "In the name of Allah, the Compassionate, the Merciful."

The author has quoted from L. Ullmann's translation, which has been newly edited with comments by L. W. Winter: The Koran, Goldmann Verlag, (Munich, 1986).

Method of quotation: 3.8 = Sura 3, verse 8.

Teaching of the Catholic Church

All the important teachings of the Church on questions of belief and morals are contained in "Denzinger"—so named after the annotator and first editor. The *Enchiridion* (Handbook) by Heinrich Denzinger first appeared in 1854, and by 1964 it was in its 32nd impression. The 1964 edition was completely reworked by Adolf Schönmetzer, so that "Denzinger" has become "Denzinger-Schönmetzer." The fact that earlier teaching documents have been eliminated from later editions not only arose from being considered obsolete; they also documented a teaching development within the Church!

A German translation of the most important Latin and Greek texts concerning the early Church can be found in "Neuner-Roos," which was brought out in 1938 by Josef Neuner and Heinrich Roos, and newly revised by Karl Rahner and Karl-Heinz Weger in 1971. The texts quoted in this book have been translated into English.

Method of quotation: the single capital letters refer to the handbooks. The number that follows does not indicate the page from which the text is taken, but the consecutive marginal numbers with which the single texts are marked.

D = H. Denzinger, Enchiridion symbolorum, definitionum et declarationum de rebus fidei et morum, 23rd impression, (Freiburg i. Br. 1937).

DS = H. Denzinger/A. Schönmetzer, Enchiridion...34th impression, (Freiburg i. Br. 1967).

NR = J. Neuner/H. Roos, "Der Glaube der Kirche in den Urkunden der Lehrverkündigung," (Regensburg, (ix) 1975).

Special Terms

Terms which have been adequately explained in the text of this book are not included here. Terms which apply to the Talmud and the Koran can be found in "Sources, Abbreviations."

Apocrypha: manuscripts which reveal many similarities with the books of the Old and New Testaments, but which were not included in the Bible. (i.e. the Thomas Evangelium, the Protoevangelium of James). Their authors wanted to fill in the gaps in the biblical accounts (e.g. Jesus's childhood) or to replace them with other writings.

Caliph: Title of the successors to Muhammad who ruled over the entire Islamic community. *Caliphate:* the domain, the rule of a Caliph. As a result of the national revival in Turkey after the First World War, the Caliphate has been abolished.

Chassidism: a Jewish mystical movement founded c. 1735 by Baal Shem-Tov. It was widely spread in Eastern Europe.

Cherub (plural: Cherubim): the name corresponds to the Babylonian *karibu,* which described the mythical beings (half animal, half human) who guarded temple and palace gates. Because of their place on the Ark of the Covenant (Ex 25.18) it was generally accepted that Yahweh reigned over the Cherubim. In the Old Testament the Cherubim announce the presence of the divine. Later they were equated with the angels, and so found their way into Christian tradition.

Christology: teaching of the person of Christ which was conceptually developed during the course of the dogmatic debates of early Christianity. The point of departure in *Evolutionary Christology* is the eternal son of God within the Trinity, and his incarnation (Christology from above), while *Transcendental Christology* (Christology from below) introduces and takes into consideration the workings and destiny of the earthly Jesus. *Adoption Christology* contains those (early Church) movements according to which Jesus is simply a human being who is made the Son of God by God ("adopted") at his baptism or resurrection.

Christological titles: the titles given to Jesus which appear in the New Testament, describing his being and his mission, and thus giving expression to belief in him. The most important titles are: Lord (Kyrios), Son of God, Christ (Messiah), Son of Man, Servant of God, Rabbi (Master, Teacher), Prophet.

Church Ban: see Excommunication.

Dogma: the truth of beliefs which are put forward and taught by the Church as binding.

Economic Salvation: God's salvational workings on mankind throughout history.

Encyclical: papal circular letter on questions of church teaching and discipline (moral behavior). The encyclicals are quoted according to their first words, which, similar to a subtitle, often point to the contents.

Eschatology: doctrine of the last things (death, judgement, resurrection, heaven, hell; of mankind: the completion of creation and of history).

Excommunication: the expulsion of a baptized Christian from the church community, thereby banning him or her from receiving the sacraments.

Exodus: the departure of God's children of Israel from Egypt. The actual Exodus starts with the crossing of the Red Sea and leads finally, through the desert, to the promised land. The memory of the Exodus has as central a significance for Jews as Easter, the feast of the Resurrection, has for Christians.

Henotheism: see Monotheism.

Hypostatic Union: union of persons. This term summarizes the teaching of the Council of Chalcedon (451), according to which Jesus Christ is true God and true Man, that is, possesses two natures, one divine and one human. Although both natures preserve their characteristics, they form a unity (union), which is born by the one divine person (Hypostasis) of the Son, which confers on Jesus's humanity its personal reality.

Incarnation: the becoming Man of the preexisting (see Preexistence) eternal Word of God (the second divine person) in Jesus Christ.

Lutherans: members of the Protestant Churches who hold fast to the Lutheran professions of faith (The Augsburg Confession among others), especially in Germany, Scandinavia and North America. Most of the Lutheran churches are amalgamated into the Lutheran World Federation (founded 1947). See Reformed Church.

Modernism: The movement within the Catholic Church from the end of the 19th century to the early 20th, which led to a crisis, particularly in France, Italy and England. It was condemned by Pius X in 1907. Its representatives tried to achieve a balance between Catholic belief and modern thinking, particularly in the fields of philosophy, historical research and biblical interpretation. The most important theses condemned had already been collected into a "Syllabus" (list) under Pius IX. In the meantime the Church has officially made its own some of the view condemned at the time (religious freedom and freedom of conscience, the chance of salvation for non-Christians, the necessity of dialogue between the Church and society and between church administration and the world).

Monotheism: strict belief in one God, which rejects both *Polytheism* (worship of many gods) and *Henotheism* (the worship of one god without denying the existence of other gods).

Preexistence: the previous existence of Jesus Christ before the Incarnation. The teaching of Jesus's preexistence states that the salvation of mankind cannot be deduced from the history of mankind, but is found in the everlasting God himself.

Rabbi: Rab: this term signifies master or teacher in the Talmud and in the New Testament. This form of address consequently developed into an honorary title, which the Palestinian teachers of the law adopted at the end of the first century A.D. The great Jewish teachers of the past were called *Rabbis,* while the Jewish servants of religion (leaders of the community) are known as *Rabbins;* their position can be compared to that of a parson or a preacher in the Protestant Free Church.

Reformed Church: this emerged from the reforms of Zwingli and Calvin. Since 1877 it has been amalgamated into the World Federation of Reformed Churches. See Lutherans.

Soteriology: the doctrine of the redemption of mankind through Jesus Christ.

Sunnites: about 90% of all Muslims are Sunnites. They form that school of thought within Islam that wishes to remain true to the "Sunna" (tradition). In 660 the *Shiites* (schia = sect, party) split away from them, recognizing Ali, the fourth Caliph and his progeny from his marriage with the Prophet's daughter Fatima, as the only legitimate leader of the whole Islamic community.

Syllabus: see Modernism.

Synod: originally synonymous with Council; in a derivative sense, an assembly of qualified members of a local church under the direction of the Bishop (Diocesan Synod). The Catholic Church has had a Synod of Bishops since 1965. It meets every two to three years, and is principally made up of representatives of the national conferences of bishops.

Synoptics: description of the evangelists Matthew, Mark and Luke, whose gospels complement each other to a large extent, thus making a synopsis (overall view) possible.

Torah: Hebrew word for "instruction" or "law." In a narrower sense in ancient Judaism it signifies the five Books of Moses (Genesis, Exodus, Leviticus, Numbers, Deuteronomy); in a wider sense the whole of the Old Testament, and frequently also the whole of Jewish religious Law.

Transcendent: that which surpasses the bounds of experience and imagination. The transcendency of God implies his "beyond the worldness" and his "difference from the world": God is simply greater than all that man can think of or say of him.

Trinity: God's three-in-oneness (one God in three persons). In the *economic theology of the Trinity* (the historical salvation), interest lies in God's salvational workings in history, while the *immanent theology of the Trinity* is concerned with God's "inner life"; that means the relationship between the three divine persons.

TIME TABLE

JUDAISM	CHRISTIANITY	ISLAM
1208-1180 B.C. Exodus from Egypt; Moses; Acquisition of land under Joshua		
1180-1004 Judges, Samuel, Saul, Beginning of the monarchy		
1004-965 David		
965-926 Solomon; division of the kingdom		
722 Decline of the north kingdom; Prophets: Hosea, Isaiah		
586-536 First destruction of Jerusalem, Babylonian exile, prophets: Jeremiah, Ezekiel. Codification of the Pentateuch		
520-420 Rebuilding of the Temple; Ezra, Nehemiah. The last prophets; Haggai, Malachi, Zechariah. Codification of prophetic writings		

JUDAISM		CHRISTIANITY	ISLAM
166-37	Maccabean rebellion. Rule of the Hasmoneans. Beginning of rabbinical learning. Spread of Judaism through dispersion and mission throughout the whole of the Mediterranean and Orient		
		7/6 B.C.-30 A.D. Life of Jesus of Nazareth	
		from c. 32 A.D. Works and missionary journeys of the Apostle Paul	
		c. 48/49 "Apostles' Council" in Jerusalem: Freedom from the Jewish Law	
		c. 64-67 Martyrdom of the Apostles Peter and Paul in Rome	
66-70 A.D.	Revolt against Rome; second destruction of Jerusalem		

JUDAISM	CHRISTIANITY	ISLAM
70-135 The Academy in Jamnia (Jabreh) becomes the spiritual center of Judaism; constitution of the Patriarchy. Pentration of Pharisaism in rabbinical Judaism.		
135-390 Rebellion of Bar-Koch-ba Collection, establishment and editing of oral tradition: edition of the Mishnah (c. 200), the Palestine Talmud (c. 390). Babylon becomes the center of rabbinical learning	c. 150 Final form of the New Testament	
	3/4 cent. Era of the great persecution of Christians	
	313 Constantine's Edict of Milan: Christianity permitted as a religion	
	380 Edict of Theodosius: Christendom the state religion	
	451 IV Ecumenical Council in Chalcedon: Christ true God and true Man	

145

JUDAISM	CHRISTIANITY	ISLAM	
500	c. 480-547		
Edition of the Babylonian Talmud	Benedict of Nursia; founder of Western Monastic rule		
		c. 570	Birth of Muhammad
		c. 613	Start of his mission
		622	Muhammad emigrates to Medina (Hegira)
		630	Conquest of Mecca
		632	Death of Muhammad
		632-661	The "four" Caliphs (Abu Bakr, Omar, Othmán and Ali)
		635	Conquest of Damascus
		638	Conquest of Jerusalem
		639-642	Conquest of Egypt and Persia. Start of conquest of North Africa
		661-750	The Omayyad Caliphate
		711-714	Conquest of Spain. Crossing of the Jaxartes (today the Syr-Darya). Invasion of the Indus valley
		732	Battle of Poitiers
		750-1258	The Abbasid Caliphate

JUDAISM		CHRISTIANITY		ISLAM	
		754	The Gift of Pepin III ("the Short") Beginning of the Papal States		
				756	The Omayyad in Spain
				762	Founding of Baghdad
				786-809	Rule of the Abbasid Caliph Harún ar-Raschid in Baghdad
		800	Imperial Coronation of Charlemagne: Beginning of the Holy Roman Empire of the German Nation		
				909	Fatimid Caliphate in North Africa
				929	The Spanish Omayyad Abd ar-Rhamán III assumes the title of Caliph
				973-1171	The Fatimids in Egypt
1000	Decline of the Schools in the Orient; Transfer of spiritual and material centers to Europe				
		1054	Definitive schism between the Eastern and Western Church		

JUDAISM		CHRISTIANITY		ISLAM	
		1077-1122	Dispute over Investitures: Discussions about the freedom of Church and State		
		1096-1270	Age of the Crusades	1096-1099	The First Crusade
				1099	The Crusaders conquer Jerusalem
				1187	Saladin reconquers Jerusalem
				1212	Battle of Las Navas de Tolosa: Start of the decline of Islamic rule in Spain
12/13 cent.	Flowering of Jewish spiritual life in Spain and France. Persecution of the Jews in France, England and Germany leads to the decline of important Jewish communities	1215	Fourth Lateran Council: Height of Papal development of power	1258	Mongolian conquest of Baghdad. End of the Abbasid Caliphate

JUDAISM	CHRISTIANITY	ISLAM
	1309-1377 "Babylonian Imprisonment" of the popes in Avignon	
	1378-1417 Western schism	
		1453 End of the Byzantine Empire: The Ottoman Turks conquer Constantinople
1492-1497 Expulsion of the Jews from the Iberian peninsula		1492 Fall of the Kingdom of Granada. End of Islamic rule in Spain
	1517 Indulgences Dispute and the beginning of the Reformation: Martin Luther	
	1522 Reformation in Zürich: Zwingli	
	1536-64 Reformation in Geneva: Calvin	
	1545-63 Council of Trent: definition of views opposed to the Reformation, internal reform of the Catholic Church	
	1555 Peace of Augsburg	

JUDAISM		CHRISTIANITY		ISLAM	
1564	Joseph Karo publishes the "Schulchan Arukh," a codex of the Jewish Ritual Law, which remains obligatory today				
End of 18th c.	Jewish Enlightenment movement starts				
				1798	Napoleon in Egypt. First contact with European science
		1869-70	Vatican Council I: primacy and infallibility of the Pope proclaimed		
		1875	Foundation of the Reformed World Federation		
19th c.	Emancipation and (relative) civil equality of the Jews in most parts of Western and Central Europe; Jewish Reform movement				
				2nd half of 19th cent.	Weakening of Ottoman rule; foundation of colonies and protectorates in Islamic territories (India, Egypt, North Africa)
1917	Balfour Declaration: during World War I England promises people of the Jewish faith a "national homeland" in Palestine			1917	Balfour Declaration
		1927	First World Church Conference "Faith and Order" in Lausanne		

JUDAISM		CHRISTIANITY		ISLAM
1940-1945	Approximately six million European Jews in Nazi Germany were murdered in the Holocaust	1947	Foundation of the Lutheran World Federation	
1948	Founding of the State of Israel	1948	First full meeting of the Ecumenical Council of Churches in Amsterdam	
		1961	First Pan-Orthodox Conference in Rhodes	
		1962-65	Vatican Council II: inner renewal and ecumenical movement of the Catholic Church	

From: E. Brunner-Traut (Ed.), "Die fünf großen Weltreligionen," Herder Verlag, (Freiburg i. Br. (xiii) 1985) pp. 87, 108, 131.